THE
Dolls' House
Wedding
BOOK

SUE JOHNSON

GUILD OF MASTER
CRAFTSMAN PUBLICATIONS

First published 2006 by Guild of Master Craftsman Publications Ltd
Castle Place, 166 High Street, Lewes, East Sussex BN7 1XU

ISBN 1 86108 451 X

Production Manager: Hilary McCallum
Managing Editor: Gerrie Purcell
Project Editor: Dominique Page
Managing Art Editor: Gilda Pacitti
Designer: Maggie Aldred

Set in Elegant Garamond BT, Swiss Light BT, Amazone BT
Colour origination by Altaimage Ltd.
Printed and bound in Singapore by Kyodo Printing Co. Ltd.

A Note About the Measurements
Most conversions are from imperial. Where accuracy is important, conversions have been
made as precise as possible. Where this is not appropriate, conversions are more approximate.
Please note that ribbons and MDF are available in the UK in standard metric sizes;
conversions to imperial are therefore approximate.

THE
Dolls' House
Wedding
BOOK

Dedication

I would like to dedicate this book to Norman,
Elizabeth and Samantha, my husband and daughters,
for their continued support, sincere encouragement
and unconditional tolerance, and to everyone
throughout my life who has believed in me despite
my reluctance to believe in myself.

*'Blessed is the influence of one true, loving
human soul on another'*

George Eliot

Foreword

To meet Sue Johnson and enter her enchanted world
is a privilege. I have been lucky enough to do so.
Sue has a talent and skill that is truly remarkable;
suddenly the world of dolls' houses, teddy bears and
miniatures come alive and the child inside the
adult mind is rekindled. I believe in the magic of this
lady, who is an artist in every sense of the word.
Without doubt, the world of dolls' houses has been
enriched by Sue and her wonderful creations.

Kathryn Russell
Bridal Designer

Contents

Introduction

I can't remember exactly when I first became interested in weddings except that I know I must have been very young. I used to pass a beautiful church on a hill as I travelled into town with my grandma each Saturday, and often I was lucky enough to catch a glimpse of a bride having her photograph taken on the steps. Like many others I'm sure, I dreamt of the day it would be my turn to dress like a princess for a day. Although it eventually came around, I didn't manage the beautiful church and my 1970's gown, which was rather plain and straight with long sleeves and a high neckline, although fashionable at the time, certainly didn't make me feel like a princess. I hasten to add, however, that the marriage turned out to be everything I'd hoped it would be. If only I'd been able to catch a glimpse of what the future held in store for me, I wouldn't have dwelt on the disappointment with my 'less-than-fairytale' wedding dress for so long. Instead, I would have looked forward with enthusiasm and anticipation to a time when I would spend many enjoyable and creative hours making fairytale wedding gowns and accessories for others, both in full size and miniature.

If asked what I thought was the best thing about dressing miniature brides, it would have to be the way in which a miniature dress is assembled. A real dress has to be made in the conventional way, following all the correct methods and rules of dressmaking; a miniature bride, however, will forgive her dressmaker if she resorts to using a little glue to fix something in to place. So, instead of making the gown first then putting it on the bride, you can make the gown around the miniature bride, adding parts separately in order to achieve the best possible creation from both the fabric and the design. This makes the whole process quicker and therefore, in some ways, more appealing, as I am able to enjoy all the intricate embroidery, beading and finishing touches that much sooner!

Over the years I have discovered a myriad of special touches which have enabled me to achieve my fairytale gowns. I have also learnt how to apply these to accessories and create some wonderful settings in which the bride can be displayed. I would like to share these with you here, and sincerely hope that you enjoy the art of miniature bridal creation.

Bridal Settings

Creating a setting in which to display your miniature bride is a fun and fulfilling pastime.

Here you will find a range of beautiful settings to make. For those who like a challenge there is a fabulous three-tiered bridal salon. But if you'd rather create a smaller setting then there is a pretty wedding garden and two delightful cameos. The cameos are especially suitable if you are just beginning to find your feet in the world of miniatures, and also make the perfect gift for a very special occasion.

Whatever your need or fancy, there is bound to be something here to help you create a really special bridal scene.

Tools and Materials

Tools

For the purpose of the settings in this section I felt it best to simply identify the contents of my own fairly limited toolbox, which, despite its size, serves me extremely well. It includes the following:

- ♥ *mitre and saw*
- ♥ *a range of clamps*
- ♥ *mini plane*
- ♥ *craft knife and assorted blades*
- ♥ *emery boards*
- ♥ *extra-fine to medium sandpaper and a sanding block*
- ♥ *mini drill and bits in various sizes*
- ♥ *set square and a quilter's grid*
- ♥ *small spirit level*
- ♥ *a set of rasps and needle files*
- ♥ *paintbrushes for fine detail as well as larger projects*
- ♥ *pencils and eraser*
- ♥ *tape measure*
- ♥ *6in (150mm) and 12in (305mm) rules*
- ♥ *metal rule*
- ♥ *wire cutters and pliers*
- ♥ *a small jig for squaring up items during construction*
- ♥ *wooden skewers for resting small painted areas of furniture*
- ♥ *toothpicks or cocktail sticks for applying small dabs of glue*
- ♥ *an awl*
- ♥ *glue spreader*
- ♥ *a painter's palette knife for applying precise amounts of wood filler or glue into awkward areas*
- ♥ *a hands-free vice.*

Power Tools

I have found that you can manage quite well at a personal level without going to the expense of purchasing power tools. But if you are becoming really serious about the hobby and would like to make miniatures at a more professional level or, indeed, many more miniatures for yourself, there are three main tools that I have found to be indispensable. These include a jigsaw for cutting MDF when fitting windows, doors and arched features; a fret saw for cutting shapes when making miniature furniture; and a mini tool such as a 'Dremel' with a range of accessories. In particular, I have found the round sanding accessory an excellent tool when shaping rounded areas. You can simulate this quite well with a piece of sandpaper wrapped around a length of dowel, or a pencil if you prefer, and a coping saw will effectively cut out spaces for windows and doors, albeit with a little more elbow grease.

Materials

The wood glue I recommend for both buildings and smaller furniture items is aliphatic resin. This product is also supplied under various trade names and there are a number of products on the market that are quite similar, so it's best just to use the full name of the glue when requesting it from your local supplier. 'Titebond' is a very good wood glue which is widely available. 'No Nails' or 'Liquid Nails' are excellent materials for plaster ware and also serve as perfect gap-fillers on light surfaces. You will need some cellulose filler for tiny gaps in plaster trims and features.

When wallpapering, I only use a dry stick glue. You can apply this glue straight to the wall, but make sure to cover every part of it before adding the paper; it is best to use a glue spreader to reach into corners and remove any 'lumps'. You will see just how easy it is to achieve a nice smooth finish without wetting the delicate papers. When redecorating at a later stage, the paper peels off with minimum effort after dampening it first with a small wet sponge.

Note

Additional materials I recommend include: wood filler, preferably in a tub rather than a tube which can prove quite a challenge when trying to squeeze the filler out if you've had it a while; a selection of masking tapes in various widths; and tailors' chalk.

The Salon

'Pumpkins and Butterflies'

This bridal salon is my pride and joy and a statement of how you can create the ultimate in luxury. As well as providing a suitable showcase for my bridal mannequins and a host of accessories, it has also enabled me to consider architectural features on a grander scale and explore the almost endless possibilities of interior design that this pastime can present. It may look a little daunting, but remember: if you take away all the decoration and furnishings from a miniature building, all you have left is a box, and anyone can make a box.

The inspiration for the name of my bridal salon came from the Charles Perrault version of the wonderful and timeless love story of *Cinderella* and her beautiful crystal coach which began that enchanted evening as a pumpkin. I was also inspired by the metamorphosis of a butterfly which represents, for me, the transformation that takes place when a bride is dressed in her wedding gown. Selecting the name was perhaps one of the most important stages, as it informed my choice of everything that followed. I chose the butterfly chairs, the Austrian crystal coach and chandeliers, the bridal slipper display unit and even some of the gowns in the salon as a result of my theme.

The construction of the bridal salon is split into four parts, as I feel it is often confusing to be presented with an avalanche of materials and dimensions at the start of a project. If, however, you prefer to have everything together at the start, simply add the material lists together. Personally, though, I have found it easier to approach very large projects in small stages.

Part 1: The Lower Floor

Before commencing with the construction of the lower floor it is important to consider the interior design, as it is necessary to decorate and illuminate certain parts before positioning them.

MATERIALS AND PREPARATION
Wallpaper, Picture Rails, Dado Trims, Cornice and Skirting

You will need the following (exact quantities depend on personal choice and pattern matching):

♥ *approx. 10 sheets of upper wallpaper*
♥ *approx. 4 sheets of central wallpaper*
♥ *approx. 8 sheets of lower wallpaper*
♥ *1 sheet of wallpaper for the recess at the back of the split-level floor*
♥ *approx. 16 lengths of 12in (305mm) plaster cornice*
♥ *approx. 16 strips each of dado, picture railing and skirting.*

As the ceilings of the salon are so high, I used three coordinating papers. The upper striped wallpaper panels are 4in (102mm) deep, the central floral panels are 10in (254mm) deep and the lower taffeta-effect paper panels are 5in (127mm) deep.

The plaster cornice I applied with the deepest 1½in (38mm) side to the wall, making the combined measurement of all four 20½in (521mm), which is the approximate height of the ceiling. (You may need to adapt the measurements to suit your choice of wallpaper.) Trim the lower wallpaper according to the height of the chosen skirting; I chose the highest skirting available.

I added picture railing to the join between the upper and central papers and dado to the join between the central and lower paper. I applied

Note

I always like to carry one or two spare lengths of mouldings for any extra decorative pieces I may wish to add later.

the border, which was cut from the central paper, to the bottom of the cornice to create a fully coordinated look.

Lighting

I decided to go for the ultimate in luxurious lighting, but you can choose alternatives if you wish. All you must remember is to choose lights that have changeable bulbs, and to position them where they can be easily reached. The spotlights don't allow bulb changing, so these have to be placed where they can be removed and replaced. The following electrical items were used:

♥ *4 six-armed crystal chandeliers*
♥ *12 matching crystal wall lights*
♥ *9 picture lights: 4 on the staircase and 5 on the upper back wall*
♥ *2 dolphin-shaped lanterns*
♥ *2 table lamps*
♥ *various pea-bulb holders, strip lights and spotlights*
♥ *5 tulip-bulb wall lights for the attic*
♥ *2 transformers, one each for the upper and lower parts of the salon*
♥ *bell wire and dolls' house wire*
♥ *4 multi-terminal connection blocks*
♥ *electrical tape.*

Wiring the Connection Box

The method I used to connect the lights was to take all the wires out through the back of the salon and connect them to multi-terminal connection blocks.

1 Insert the two wires from the transformer into terminals 13 and 14.

2 Loop short pieces of bell wire from 14 to 16, 16 to 18, 18 to 20, 20 to 22, 22 to 24 then, from 13 to 15, 15 to 17, 17 to 19, 19 to 21, and 21 to 23. This runs your current through the transformer and along the length of the block.

3 When adding a second connection block using the same transformer, take further bell wire from 23 on this block to 13 on the next then join the other terminals as before.

4 Take the next row from 24 on this block to 14 on the next block. Remember not to exceed the number of bulbs each transformer is intended for. I always purchase a transformer with a high bulb capacity. For the salon I bought two transformers, each intended for up to 64 bulbs.

Adding the Lights

1 As a general guide when using the connection block method, take one wire from two or three lights and twist them together before securing them into terminal 1.

2 Take the remaining wire from each of the lights, twist them together and insert them into the terminal 2, and so on. It is essential to keep the two sets of wires from each light apart. The reason for twisting the wires from two or three lights at a time is just to ensure a good connection, as the miniature lights have such fine wire.

3 Continue along the block in this way.

Note

If you are not familiar with electrical rules and procedures, please have your work checked by someone who is.

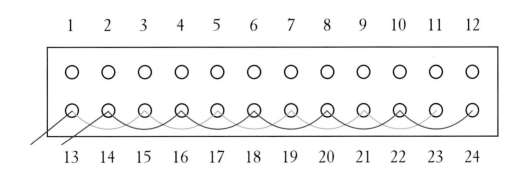

Features and Fittings

I have used only the finest features and fittings, as they were bought for me as gifts, but they can be replaced with less expensive options if you prefer. I used the following items:

- ♥ *4 hanging ceiling light roses*
- ♥ *2 shell niches*
- ♥ *2 sets of 6 dolphin balusters and 2 top and bottom rails*
- ♥ *2 medium plaster plinths for the dolphin lanterns*
- ♥ *4 large plaster plinths for the upper floor and 4 column bases for displays*
- ♥ *2 half plaster plinths and 2 half column tops and bottoms for the barley twist ceiling supports at the front of the lower floor*
- ♥ *1 plaster dolphin fountain and pool*
- ♥ *2 plaster bird tables for the large floral displays*
- ♥ *a selection of smaller urns, stands, small columns and statuettes according to personal taste*
- ♥ *10 pineapple finials, including the two for the attic pediment*
- ♥ *decorative plaques and plaster rosettes*
- ♥ *3 pairs of cherub corbels*
- ♥ *4 ready-made 12in (305mm) baluster railings; I used these for the upper floor stairwells as they made the perfect depth with the edge of the stair support for a single neat ¾in (19mm) square post.*

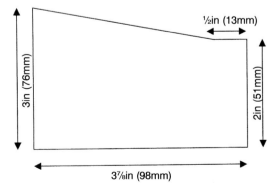

½in (13mm)

3in (76mm)

2in (51mm)

3⅞in (98mm)

You will need to cut the following:
from ⅜in (9mm) MDF:

Split-level floor:
   48in wide x 10in deep (1219 x 254mm)

Inner wall room divides x 2:
   18½in high x 10in wide (470 x 254mm)

Stair support inner sides x 2:
   18½in high x 2¾in wide (470 x 70mm)

Recess step:
   7in wide x 3½in deep (178 x 89mm)

Using diagram F on page 23 as a guide, cut two stair supports to form the integral banisters.

Using the diagram on the left, cut two outer sides for the dolphin baluster rails.

Cut the following from ½in (12mm) MDF:

Base:
   54in wide x 30in deep (1372 x 762mm)

Inner floors x 2:
   48in wide x 23½in deep (1219 x 597mm)

Sides x 2:
   42in high x 24in wide (1067 x 610mm)

Back:
   42in high x 48in wide (1067 x 1219mm)

Upper ceiling:
   49in wide x 24in deep (1245 x 610mm)

First flight of steps for staircases x 2:
   5½in wide x 14in deep (140 x 356mm)
   5½in wide x 13in deep (140 x 330mm)
   5½in wide x 12in deep (140 x 305mm)
   5½in wide x 11in deep (140 x 280mm)
   5½in wide x 10in deep (140 x 254mm)
   5½in wide x 9in deep (140 x 229mm)
   5½in wide x 8in deep (140 x 203mm)
   5½in wide x 7in deep (140 x 178mm)

5½in wide x 6in deep (140 x 152mm)

5½in wide x 5in deep (140 x 127mm)

Staircase landings x 2:

4in wide x 8⅝in deep (101 x 219mm)

First step of second flight of staircases x 2:

2¾in wide x 6in deep (70 x 152mm)

Steps for second flight of staircases x 10:

2¾in wide x 3½in deep (70 x 89mm)

Lower ceiling support:

20⁹⁄₁₆in high x 48in wide (522 x 1219mm)

Cut the following from ¾in(18mm) MDF:

Three steps leading to the split-level floor:

Lower step 9½in wide x 4½in deep (241 x 114mm)

Middle step 7½in wide x 3½in deep (190 x 89mm)

Top step 5½in wide x 2½in deep (140 x 64mm)

You will also need:

♥ *carpet*

♥ *2¾in (70mm) wide stair units x 2*

♥ *½in (13mm) handrail with a ⅜in (9mm) rebate for the two stair support features*

♥ *½in (13mm) square stripwood and two caps for the banister posts on the landing*

♥ *¾in (19mm) square stripwood and twelve caps for the banister and display posts on the upper floor and under the pineapple finials at the bottom of the two staircases and the landing post*

♥ *⅛in (3mm) jelutong sheet wood x 2½in (64mm) and 3in (76mm) widths*

♥ *⅜ x ¼in (10 x 6mm) stripwood*

♥ *2 strips of small-scale half-round moulding for the trims under the dolphin rails plus 2 tiny corbels for under the cap at the bottom of the two staircases*

♥ *2 x 1in (51 x 25mm) smooth ready-planed timber with a finished size of approximately*

Note

If you are having the wood cut for you it may be easier to request a rear lower ceiling support that is 20½in (520mm) high, depending upon the accuracy of the cutting tool in use. You can then add ½ x ⅛in (12 x 2mm) stripwood, readily available from a miniature wood supplier, as I did.

1¾ x ¾in (38 x 12mm) to form the underside of the split-level floor

♥ *2 arched interior windows*

♥ *2 laser-cut decorative arches*

♥ *decorative flat-backed barley-twist wood strip for the front lower ceiling supports*

♥ *quick-drying white primer and two exterior paints in your chosen colours: a main colour and a secondary colour trim*

♥ *liquid gold leaf.*

I have used the 'Dulux' range of 1822 period emulsion in the following areas:

Exterior:

Porcelain Blue for the walls and Regency White for the trims

Ceilings:

Rose Pink

Reverse sides of the split-level floor inner wall divides and the recess panels:

Sung Blue (which is a pale green shade)

Front edges of MDF floors and sides:

Camisole Pink

1 Glue your first inner floor to the base of the salon, using **A** as a guide for placement. Apply weight as the glue dries, paying particular attention to the corners and edges. Use clamps where possible.

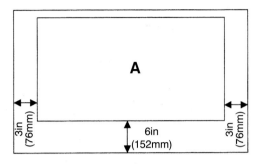

> *Tip*
> ♥
>
> If you are constructing the salon onto a stand as I did, it is best to prime and paint the side edges and front edge of the base in your secondary exterior paint colour at this point so that you don't mark any decorative trim around the stand. I have used Camisole Pink for this to blend in with the carpeting. (Plans for the stand are available from me at the address on page 188.)

2 Glue the left-hand side of the salon into place together with the back of the salon (**B**). You can use off-cuts of MDF to keep the corner square. I also find my quilters' grid an excellent tool for squaring up those corners. Tape the side and back corner securely and leave until dry.

3 Glue the rear lower ceiling support flat to the back of the salon, applying glue to the left-hand edge and the lower edges as well as the surface to be glued to the back.

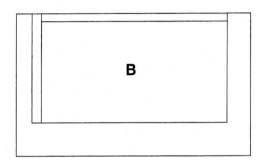

> *Tip*
> ♥
>
> At this stage I find it a little easier to work on the split-level flooring before adding the second side. You can then glue the completed construction into place without scraping glue from the edges onto the inner sides of the salon. It does, however, require you to be exact when cutting the floor supports; they must not protrude on the right-hand side of the back and bottom inner floor by even a fraction of a millimetre.

4 Cut and glue the narrow side of two long pieces of planed 2 x 1in (51 x 25mm) timber to the back and front of the split-level floor (which will then become the underside) and two shorter pieces to the sides, using **C** as a guide. The narrower side of the timber is the edge that is glued to the surface of the floor. Clamp and add weight to the structure whilst it is drying.

5 Apply glue to the four lower edges of the timber and the left-hand side and back edges of the floor unit. Firmly and squarely glue the unit into place at the back of the salon.

6 Glue the right-hand side of the salon onto the structure, applying glue to the right-hand side of the split-level floor unit, the right side edge of the back of the salon and the lower edge of the right-hand side itself. You can also apply a little glue to the side edges of the bottom inner floor. Tape the entire structure at the back to ensure everything dries squarely and securely.

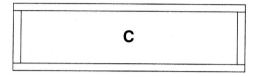

C

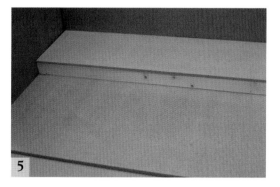

5

7

7 Begin building up your first staircase with the ten steps that form the first flight using the corner of the salon to keep them nice and square as you progress. Allow to dry.

Note

At this stage, begin building the two staircases, but they are not to be glued into position on the split-level floor; the supporting stair structure and inner wall room divides will keep them securely in place. I used these two structures as well as an MDF off-cut to help position the steps during their construction.

8

8 Using a ⅜in (9mm) MDF off-cut flush with the edge of the split-level floor as a guide to position the steps (this is where the inner wall room divides will be), add the landing but do not glue it in place yet. Position and glue the first step of the second flight into place on the landing. Continue adding and gluing the final five steps with a tread depth of ¾in (19mm).

9 Make up the second first flight of steps and construct an opposite landing and second flight using the first structure to help with the positioning of the steps.

10 Cut out the holes for the interior windows in the inner wall divides using **D** as a guide. Draw around the inner frame of the window and drill a hole in the bottom right-hand corner large enough for the saw that you are using. You may need to make another hole half way around the arch to help guide your saw smoothly round it (**E**). Do not glue the window in place until you have decorated the wall.

11 Using **F** as a guide, cut out the holes for the two niches in the stair supports. Insert all the components and the staircases and check their positioning. Glue the two landings and second flight of steps into position on the top tread, making sure everything is snug, square and even. Again, remember you are not gluing the staircases to the wall itself; they will stand in position quite well due to their weight.

12 Sand any protruding areas on the stair supports and draw an outline around the ten steps of the first flight of stairs onto the actual stair support. This will help you when you add the decoration. Remove all components.

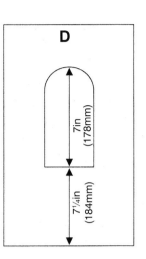

D

7in (178mm)

7¼in (184mm)

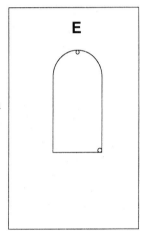

E

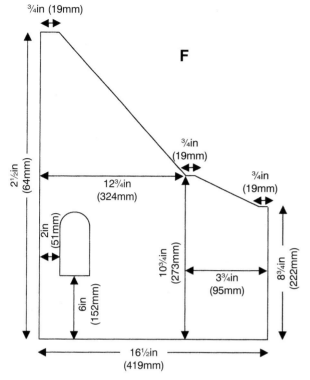

¾in (19mm)

F

2½in
(64mm)

2in
(51mm)

6in
(152mm)

¾in
(19mm)

12¾in
(324mm)

10¾in
(273mm)

¾in
(19mm)

3¾in
(95mm)

8¾in
(222mm)

16½in
(419mm)

13

13 Cut a 5½in (140mm) strip of carpet and begin carpeting the first flight of the staircase, starting from the bottom. You will need an extra ½in (13mm) width at the top of the stairs to take the carpet right up to the beginning of the first step of the second flight. Take a strip of carpet 4in (102mm) wide from here to the back of the first step. Cut a third strip 2¾in (70mm) wide and apply it to the remaining steps on the second flight. Repeat for the opposite staircase and then carpet the two stair units, leaving the top riser and tread until carpeting the upper floor.

14 Measure at the front two sides of the salon, 20⁹⁄₁₆in (522mm) from the floor for your ceiling height. With the inner wall divides in place, draw a ceiling line from the mark you have made along to the top of the wall divide then to the top of the rear lower ceiling support. Place your cornice on this line and draw a line under the cornice. Continue around the corner of the rear lower ceiling support and on the front of the inner wall divide. Repeat for the opposite side.

15 Measure 8½in (216mm) from the rear left-hand side corner of the salon along the top of the rear lower ceiling support and mark with a pencil. This is where the stairwell will begin. Draw a vertical line up the back edge of the inner wall divide, on the side of the salon itself, ensuring the line you draw is at a 90-degree angle with the floor. You will use this line to begin wallpapering the landing. Repeat at the opposite side then remove all the components and staircases.

23

16 Cut two widths of wallpaper of the design that is to be positioned above the picture rail and below the cornice in the remainder of the salon. One needs to be 9⅝in (244mm) wide to cover from the pencil line behind the inner wall divide to the corner. The other needs to be 8½in (216mm) wide and cover the back wall from the corner to the beginning of the stairwell, leaving the height of the wallpaper as it is supplied. Make sure to match the wallpaper. Apply the paper approximately ½in (13mm) down from the cornice line you have drawn, beginning it on the vertical line at the back of the inner wall divide. The reason for applying it so far down is so that the bottom of the sheet falls below the top step of the first flight of the staircase. The height of standard wallpaper strips is usually 11½in (292mm).

17 Place a pencil mark on the rear lower ceiling support 20½in (521mm) from the corner. This is where the end of the stairwell will fall. Position the stair unit up to this line and mark where the unit will end. Cut a piece of the wallpaper with full height to a width which will just clear the stair unit and glue it into position so that the top of the sheet is level with the rear lower ceiling support. Repeat for the opposite side.

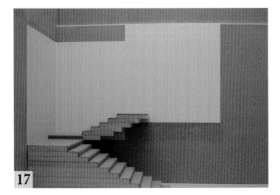

17

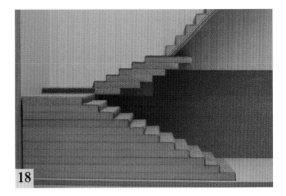

18

18 With the main staircases in place, apply glue to the inner side of the stair units and fit them into position, making sure that the tops will be level with the upper floor. You can use a 7in (178mm) wide off-cut of ½in (12mm) MDF lined up in the centre of the upper floor with 20½in (521mm) on both sides of it to indicate where the stairwell ends, to help you position the stair units.

19 Cut the border from your main wallpaper and apply it below the cornice line with mitred corners. The border should go up the side of the cornice line at the start of the stairwell and along the top of the rear lower ceiling support to the stair unit position. Repeat for the opposite side. (See photograph at top of page 25.)

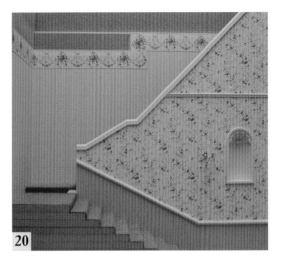

20

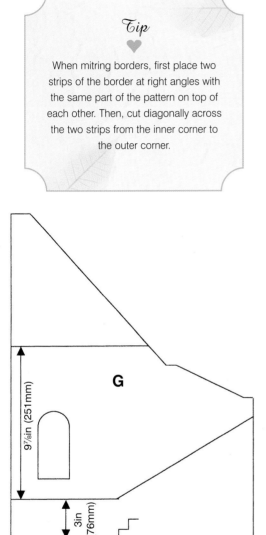

G

9⅞in (251mm)

3in (76mm)

20 Decorate the stair supports using **G** as a guide. First fit and cut but do not glue the rebated handrail to the upper edge, making sure to angle the cuts correctly where the pieces follow the lines of the upper edge. Remove each piece in turn and label the underside so that you know where they fit. I labelled mine L (left) 1–5 and R (right) 1–5. Prime and paint each piece and leave to dry.

21 To work out the slope for the paper below the dado rail, first draw a 3in (76mm) line up from the bottom of the support, starting at the tallest side and ending at the start of the steps you drew earlier, making sure that you stop up from the step at a 90-degree angle. Lay your ruler parallel with the outer tips of the stair treads you drew and draw a slope up from the top of the 3in (76mm) line. Cut your wallpaper accordingly. The middle section is the height of the main wallpaper with the border removed or 10in (254mm) deep. The top section I chose to keep simple, as it comes up within the upper floor. All wallpapers and mouldings were trimmed flush at both sides of each stair support. The picture rail and dado rails were primed and painted with Regency White paint and placed over the joins. I painted the back of the stair supports with Sung Blue leaving ⅜in (10mm) down the edge of the tallest side where the stair support inner sides are to be glued. Use a strip of masking tape to maintain a clean edge. Add the rebated handrail to the upper edge, filling any tiny gaps with filler before adding a final touch up with paint over the joins. Glue the niches into place.

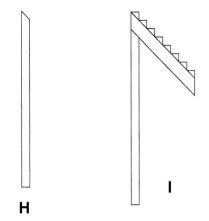

H

I

22 Chamfer the upper corners of the stair support inner sides as shown in **H**. Position them under the stair units and sand the chamfered edge until you have a snug fit (**I**). Glue the inner sides to the stair supports, making sure to fit them the correct way to support each stair unit.

23 Prime and paint the windows and their reverse facings for the inner wall divides then allow to dry. Paint the reverse side of the divides; I used Sung Blue after an initial coat of primer. Decorate the front once the paint is dry. Cut a strip of upper wallpaper 4in (102mm) deep and apply below the cornice line that you drew in Step 14. I left a little wallpaper at the side of the divide, which is to be glued onto the side of the salon to fit around the corner when the divide is in place. Cut around the arch with a sharp craft knife. Add the 10in (254mm) deep strip of floral paper and again, cut around the arch. Glue the windows, glazing and facings into position and add primed and painted picture rails and dado trim.

24 Begin testing the lights you are going to need. To do this safely, always test with the transformer, placing the two pins of the light plug onto the terminals of the transformer. If the light is not working, first check that the bulbs are not loose before replacing them with new bulbs. Test the two chandeliers and after testing the dolphin lanterns, paint them with liquid gold leaf and glue them to the plinths. Finally, test the following lights for installation at this stage:

♥ 6 crystal wall lights, one for the outer side of each niche on the stair supports and one on each side of the arched window on the wall divides

♥ 4 picture lights, one in the centre of each landing on the back wall and one more above the arched windows on the back of the wall divides.

25 Take the wire from the landing picture lights straight through the back of the salon. Drill a hole under each staircase and guide the wire from the niche crystal wall lights through there. Apply glue to the inner edge of the stair support sides, the lower edge of the structure and a small spot to each tread of the stair units before manoeuvring the structure into place. Repeat for the opposite side.

27 Keeping the three wires from the first wall divide lights together, apply glue to the inner edge of the wall divide which is to be joined to the side of the salon and to the lower edge. Whilst allowing the wires to lie freely down the staircase, press the divide firmly into position against the side of the salon. You can use masking tape from the outer tip at the top of the divide, up and over the top of the salon walls to hold the divide in place. After installing the second divide in the same way, I also used a length of stripwood between the two divides to hold them firmly against the sides of the salon. Use another length of masking tape across the top of the two sides of the salon itself to keep everything nice and square.

26 Cut the chamfered edge from one side of a ½in (13mm) cap and place it at the base of the left-hand side of the left stair support on the landing so that the cut edge of the cap is next to the step. Make a pencil mark where the ⅜in (9mm) side of the support ends and cut the corner of the cap so that it sits perfectly flush. Cut a length of ½in (13mm) square stripwood level with the top of the handrail and remove both the cap and post. Glue the cap to the base of the post then prime and paint the post, leaving a strip of bare wood down the middle of the side, which is to be glued to the stair support. Paint a ¾in (19mm) cap and glue it to the top of the post partly over the handrail. Glue a pineapple finial to the top. Make a second post for the right stair support landing.

28 Cut four lengths of cornice with mitred corners to fit the side and back of the landings. Use an off-cut of MDF across the top of the wall divide and the rear lower ceiling support to act as a faux ceiling and glue the four pieces of cornice into position, applying glue only to the back of the cornice that is to be adhered to the wall. Use cellulose filler for any gaps in the corners of the cornice.

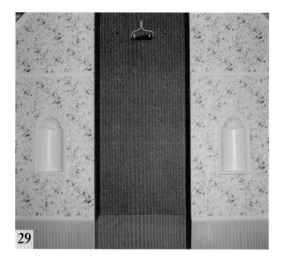

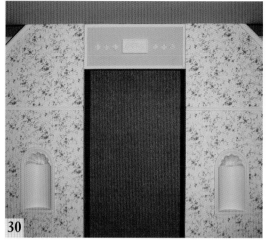

29 Wallpaper the recess at the centre of the stair supports with your chosen paper; I chose a deep rose marbled paper to provide a suitable background colour for my Swarovski crystal coach and butterfly. At the top of the recess just below the ceiling line I installed a striplight to illuminate the crystals. The light first required a bell wire connection that had been soldered on to the metal rings at each side of the light as they are supplied without the wiring attached, unlike other dolls' house lighting. Alternatively, you can install wired bulb holders in their place. I drilled a small round hole on each side of the striplight to house two round bulb holders for extra light. All three wires went straight out the back of the salon.

30 Cut a piece of 3 x ⅛in (76 x 3mm) sheet wood the width of the recess for the upper panel. Prime and paint with your chosen paint (I have used Sung Blue), leaving a small border around the edge to glue on some picture-rail moulding which I had cut with mitred corners, primed then painted with Regency White paint. Add the moulding using clamps at the corners. When dry I added a plaster plaque to the centre with three rosettes on each side before gluing the completed panel into place at the top of the recess.

31 Position the bottom dolphin baluster rail in place at the base of the first step of the staircases next to the lantern plinths and draw around it. Remove the rails and assemble them with the handrails and dolphin balusters using 'No Nails' adhesive. Make sure to have the outer edges of the rails in line.

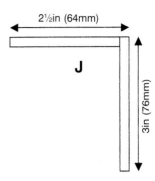

32

34

32 Drill a small hole at the centre of the recess at the bottom to feed the wires from the lanterns through to the back of the salon. With the plinths in place, take the wires loosely down from the lanterns at the back and tape in place. Allow for a little movement so that you can carpet the split-level floor. Feed the wires loosely through the drilled hole. Cut two lengths of ½in (13mm) square stripwood, each 3½in (89mm) long. Glue one in each rear corner at the bottom of the recess.

33 Carpet the split-level floor. Cut a rough rectangle of carpet to fit that area. Place a right angle of carpet in the rear corner at the base of the first staircase. Take the back straight edge of the carpet straight across the recess, over the lantern wires and up to the base of the second staircase. At the front, cut the carpet along the edge of the rail outline and carefully under or around the plinths to the front edge. I chose to fit the carpet under the plinths, as I didn't want to glue them to the wooden floor in case the lanterns required any work or replacement at a later date. The carpet also offers some adhesion for the plinths to stand on.

34 Cut a front panel for the lower display shelf in the recess from the 3 x ⅛in (76 x 3mm) sheet wood to fit just inside the bottom of the recess. Cut a piece of 2½ x ⅛in (64 x 3mm) sheet wood the same width and glue the two together, as shown in diagram **J**. I painted the top surface in Regency White and the front panel in Sung Blue, leaving a narrow border to glue on some picture rail moulding with mitred corners as for the upper recess panel. I added a plaster rose plaque to the centre of the front panel and saved two more for the outer panels at the side of the dolphin baluster rails. The image shows how the display shelf will look on top of the recess step, with the lanterns, step and rails in place. You will complete these features and decor at a later stage.

35 Cover the recess step with carpet including the two sides, which will protrude at the front of the recess. Place the step in the recess up to the stripwood and position the lower recess display unit on top of the step, allowing the back of the unit to rest on the ½in (13mm) square stripwood corner posts. There is no need to glue the display shelf into position, as it will rest quite securely by itself as well as allowing access to the wiring if you should need it. Add skirting to both sides of the recess, cutting it out to fit snugly on top of the first step.

36 Cut a half circle display shelf from ⅛in (3mm) sheet wood using **K** as a guide. Glue a cherub corbel support to the centre of the underside and, when dry, prime and paint the shelf. Glue into position at the centre of the back of the recess so that the arched panels, once in place, will nicely frame the object you choose for the shelf. This will take a little forward planning but the shelf needs to be in place before the arched panels are installed.

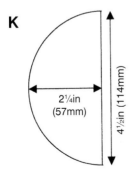

K

2¼in (57mm)

4½in (114mm)

37

37 Paint the laser-cut arch panels. Cut two lengths of dado moulding to fit from under the upper recess panel down to the top of the recess step. Cut away or sand the centre of the moulding at the upper part of the strip to the height of the arched panels, so that they can be glued to a flat surface. Glue the panels to the dado strips and paint the remaining surfaces of each structure. Glue the moulding and arch structures to the front edges of the recess.

38 Position the dolphin baluster rails and chamfer the top edge of the handrail so that it sits neatly under the upper rim around the plinth. Glue the railings in place and use cellulose filler for any gaps.

39 Cut two lengths of ⅜ x ¼in (10 x 6mm) stripwood the height of the inner wall divides, prime and paint, leaving the side bare which is to be glued to the edge of the divide. Glue into place.

40

42

40 Paint the two MDF outer sides of the railings. I painted them in Sung Blue with a Regency White top edge. Add the plaster rose plaques and glue them into position with the dolphin baluster structures. Paint and glue a ¾in (19mm) cap over the sides and railing with a tiny corbel as a support feature and add a pineapple finial to the top.

41 Complete the wallpaper décor around the two sides of the salon as started on the wall divides, cutting a 5in (127mm) strip of the lower wallpaper. Paint sufficient picture rails, dado moulding and skirting before fitting, then fill any tiny gaps and joins with white filler before painting over them. Carpet the entire lower floor. Fill any gaps in plaster features with cellulose filler.

42 Cut the sides of the half column tops straight where they are to be placed next to the cornice. Mark the width of your half column top at the front edge of the salon where the cornice will end. Apply the border all the way around under the cornice line you drew earlier. At the front edge of the salon where the column top will be, take the border upwards to the ceiling line. Mitre the corner at the front edge. Do not add the cornice until the ceiling is in place. This image shows how it will eventually look (with the cornice in place).

43 Glue into place at the front edge of the salon, the half plinth with the half column bottom above it. Measure the height from the top of these two features to the ceiling line. Subtract the height of the half column top and cut a length of half barley twist to fit between. Prime and paint the barley twist before gluing into position with the column top.

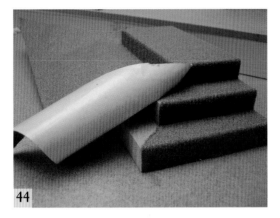

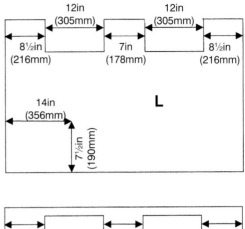

12in
(305mm)

12in
(305mm)

8½in
(216mm)

7in
(178mm)

8½in
(216mm)

14in
(356mm)

7½in
(190mm)

L

8½in
(216mm)

7in
(178mm)

8½in
(216mm)

M

44 Glue and carpet the three steps that lead up to the split-level floor. First lay a piece of carpet on the top step, flush with the back of the steps. Make sure you have sufficient carpet on both sides to reach the bottom. Bring the carpet down each side and smooth into place on each step. Cut the carpet diagonally at the outer corner of every tread and straight down at the end of each riser. Smooth the carpet down each step at the front, cutting the corners as before. To make sure you don't cut off too much, first feel the ridge at every corner with your fingertips and cut carefully a little at a time using your fingertips as a guide. Place the steps in position. There is no need to glue them in place.

45 Add a thin painted strip of small-scale half-round moulding along the upper edge of the split-level floor below the dolphin railings from the wood strip down the edge of the inner wall divide along to the three steps leading up to the split-level floor.

46 Prepare the ceiling, using **L** as a guide. I chose to cut the stairwells out entirely from the edge as I planned to install planting to disguise the rear lower ceiling support. You can opt to cut out the stairwells, leaving ½in (13mm) at the far side of the stairwell (**M**) if you do not want this feature.

47 Position the ceiling in its resting place in the salon. Draw a pencil line along the top where the inner wall divides are and remove the ceiling.

48 Mask just inside the following areas before painting, so there are no gaps between them and the paintwork:

❤ the area where the top of the inner wall divides are to be glued to the ceiling

❤ the area where the cornice is to be glued: in front of the wall divides and at the sides of the salon

❤ the back of the ceiling which is to rest on the rear lower ceiling support.

49 Mark the position of the chandeliers using diagram **L** as a guide. Measure the diameter of your ceiling roses and, using a compass, draw a circle that is slightly smaller, again to ensure that there are no gaps, placing the point of the compass on the initial mark you made. Drill a hole on this mark. Prime the entire unmasked surface, leaving the circles bare where the ceiling roses are to be glued. You will need two coats of colour; I used Rose Pink for the ceilings. Remove the masking tape as soon as you have given the ceiling its second coat and before the paint dries. I gave the front edge two coats of Camisole Pink.

50 Drill a small hole 2½in (63mm) from the side behind where the inner wall divides will be. This is through which to feed the three wires from the inner wall divide lights.

51 Glue the ceiling rose into position, making sure it is central over the hole for the light. Use some thin wire or thin wood dowel if you need help. Thread the chandelier wire up the centre of the rose and ceiling then tape it to hold the chandelier in place. You can thread the chandeliers through after fitting the ceiling if you find it easier.

52 Apply glue to the following places: on top of the rear lower ceiling support where parts of the ceiling are to fall, missing out the stairwell spaces where the plants are to go if you chose this feature; the top of the inner wall divides; and the side and back edges of the ceiling. I added some 'No Nails' to the top of the plaster cornice above the landings. Carefully lower the ceiling into position to reduce the possibility of smearing any glue. Run a long length of masking tape from one side of the salon at the ceiling line to the other side. Add the four pieces of cornice with mitred corners in front of the inner wall divides and to each side up to the half column tops at the front of the salon.

53 On the upper floor, drill a hole large enough to take several wires 4in (102mm) from each side wall at floor level on the back wall. Guide the three wires at the back of the divides up through the hole in the ceiling you drilled after painting it, using a length of wire as a leader to pull them through one by one. Feed these three wires at either side out through the holes to the back of the salon. Guide the chandelier wires out to the back of the salon through the same hole. The display podiums on the upper floor will sit on top of these wires so that they are all concealed neatly. As well as being very decorative, this particular feature allows for easy access if you wish to add further lighting at a later date. To conceal the wires further, you can either form a small channel in the floor into which you lay the wires or you can use tape to lay them as flat as possible on the floor surface. You can begin wiring up the lighting from the lower floor using either your own method or the multi-terminal connection method outlined earlier on page 17.

Part 2: The Upper Floor

There are certain essential matters to consider when constructing the upper floor. Chiefly, the features need to offer support to such a high and wide ceiling. Technically, the ceiling of a large space without wall divides requires a solid support, as wood can bow. The attic plinth adhered to the upper-floor ceiling will create a certain amount of stability and help prevent sagging, but this still leaves a large centre front area which could sag over time. Therefore, a second feature which you may like to install is a pair of columns just behind the chandeliers and towards the centre of the ceiling. You must remember, though, that if inserting columns on the upper floor, you must also install two further columns below them, but not directly below – somewhere within a circumference of 2–3in (51–76mm), and towards the sides rather than the centre to maintain the aesthetic quality of the salon. The ready-made miniature columns that are available are not tall enough; an alternative, though, is to use readily available plaster plinths and the column top and bottom sections only.

The usual ready-made 12in (305mm) column itself can be replaced either with lengths of fluted dowel or with full round barley twist to continue the theme, with an approximate diameter of 1in (25mm) cut to the desired height according to your choice of plinth. I have chosen not to insert columns in order to maximize display space. I once inserted them below a similar area in my dolls' house and found years later that the columns can still be moved and the ceiling has not sagged at all. This doesn't mean that it won't ever sag, it's just something you need to be aware of.

MATERIALS AND PREPARATION

♥ *Make up and paint four half-round display shelves, as instructed in Step 36 of the salon lower floor construction, or five if you do not want a painting in the centre gap. The back of the shelf needs to be slightly narrower, measuring 3½in (89mm) and using a compass set at half this width, the depth of the shelf should be 1¾in (44mm).*

♥ *Cut 4in (102mm) deep strips of upper wallpaper.*

♥ *Trim 10in (254mm) deep strips of floral wallpaper.*

♥ *Cut 5in (127mm) deep strips of lower wallpaper.*

♥ *Mitre four pieces of cornice to fit in the two rear corners. You will also need four straight lengths and a short piece.*

♥ *Paint sufficient picture rails, dado, skirting and the four ready-made baluster rails for the stairwells and display sides, making sure not to paint the edges that will be glued to the posts.*

♥ *Test the following lights: 6 crystal wall lights, 5 picture lights, 2 chandeliers and 2 table lights.*

♥ *Cut four lengths of ³⁄₄in (18mm) stripwood 2³⁄₄in (70mm) long for the four railing posts. Cut one chamfered edge from four of the caps and glue one to the bottom of each post. Glue the remaining four full caps to the top of the posts then add the pineapple finials.*

♥ *You will need a small piece of ¹⁄₂in (12mm) square stripwood, ³⁄₃₂ x ³⁄₈in (2.5 x 9mm) stripwood, ¹⁄₂ x ¹⁄₁₆in (12 x 1.5mm) stripwood, dried flower oasis and plants for the two stairwell plant boxes if you have the lower floor ceiling shown in diagram* **N**.

You will also need to cut the following from ¹⁄₂in (12mm) MDF:

Attic plinth:
> 51in wide x 25¹⁄₂in deep (1295 x 648mm)

Cut the following from ³⁄₄in (18mm) MDF for the two corner display podiums:

Base x 2:
> 8¹⁄₂in wide x 11in deep (216 x 279mm)

Middle rear step x 2:
> 8¹⁄₂in wide x 3³⁄₄in deep (216 x 95mm)

Small steps x 4:
> 4¹⁄₄in wide x 3³⁄₄in deep (108 x 95mm)

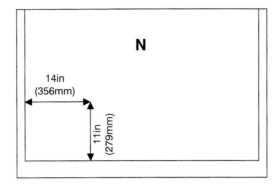

1 Centre and glue the ceiling on the attic plinth so they are flush at the back. You will see that there is a deeper border at the front edge compared with the sides – this is to allow for the façade door. Mark out and drill the holes for the upper floor chandeliers using **N** as a guide. Make sure to measure from the front of the ceiling and not the plinth. Note that the chandeliers on this floor are set a little further back as there are no inner wall divides on this floor. Prepare and paint the ceiling as for the lower floor ceiling in Step 49 on page 33, masking the back of the ceiling and the two sides where the cornice is to go. Add the ceiling roses and chandeliers as in Step 51 (page 33).

2 Apply glue to the upper three edges of the back and sides of the salon and lift the ceiling and plinth structure into place. Take care, as the structure is quite heavy. Tape securely with wide masking tape at the back and, using the same tape, pull lengths tightly from above the plinth and down the sides.

3 Fit the cornice around the back and sides then add the wallpaper, picture railing and finally the dado mouldings.

4 Install the crystal wall lights 13in (330mm) from floor level with the two lights at the outside of the row 6½in (165mm) from the corner and a 7in (178mm) space between them and each of the others. Now glue the shelves centrally between them.

5 You may like to decide upon the displays you would like on your shelves before installing the picture lights to ensure that you have sufficient height between the surface of the shelves and the picture light above them.

6 If you have inserted the floor shown in N, cut and trim two short pieces of ½in (13mm) square stripwood the depth of the top tread of the upper stair unit and glue it into position at the side of the tread. Make a flower box: Cut a length of stripwood for the base 11¼in (286mm) long. Check it will fit snugly in the stairwell space. Cut two ½ x ¹⁄₁₆in (13 x 1.5mm) lengths of stripwood and glue them to the back and front of the base with two ⅜ x ³⁄₃₂in (10 x 2.5mm) lengths at each side. Make another box for the other side then prime and paint in your chosen colour. I have used Rose Pink. Fill with dried flower oasis and apply a coat of thinned acrylic paint to the surface. Allow to fully dry before adding your plants. I have chosen some handmade ivy sprigs, lavender and paper roses together with five fronds of some commercially bought Yucca plants, which I first separated from the wooden stem. For the time being, put the boxes to one side.

6

7 If using self-adhesive carpet, apply the first sheet centrally, starting at the front of the floor. Apply a second sheet to the left of this and a third sheet to the right. Place the right-hand side of a fourth sheet up to the edge of the second sheet and make a fold at the wall edge. Trim and apply the strip and repeat for the other side.

8 Fit a final piece of carpet flush at the top of the stairs between the posts and across each side to cover the top treads of the stair units and the small block at the side, if you have used this feature, then the riser below the top tread and the front of the block beside it.

9 Install the optional table lights at the outer corners of the room, leaving sufficient wire to enable them to be placed above the podiums on a side table.

10 Make up the display podiums. Glue a middle rear step on top of each base flush at the back. Carpet this structure separately, covering the top and the front of the riser below it, the side that will be on view and the front edge or riser. Remember, the sides you cover will be in reverse for the two podiums. Position the podium bases into the two corners.

10

11

11 Carpet the top of the four small steps, once again covering the top and the two sides that are to be on view and again in reverse for each podium. Place the smaller steps in position on the podiums.

12

14

12 Place one of the posts in situ at the front of the middle rear step at the side of the stairwell with the cut side of the bottom post cap against the step. Measure and cut a piece of railing to fit between the wall and the post. Glue the railing to the post only. The other side of the railing is just to rest against the wall. This railing needs to be flush with the side of the post on the podium. Remove and paint the post before installing this feature as a freestanding structure to allow for easy removal of the podium. Now repeat for the opposite side.

13 Measure and fit a length of skirting at the centre back of the floor between the top two treads of the stairs and position the flower boxes in place at the back of the stairwell on top of the rear lower ceiling support. There shouldn't be a need to glue the boxes into position, as you will find they fit quite snugly after adding the carpet to the front edge of the little block. I'm also very much an advocate of keeping some features semi-permanent, if possible, to allow for future additions or changes. Cut and fit two further pieces of skirting on the side walls in front of the podiums.

14 Position full lengths of baluster railing in front of the stairwells. Carefully cut a small strip of carpet where they are to stand. Apply glue to the bottom of the rails only and use another post pressed against each in turn at the stair support edge to ensure a snug fit. Tape the post in place until the railing has set, then remove the post for painting. Try to leave the small area on one side of the post bare where the railing and stair support is to be glued to it. You can touch up these areas once the post is in position. It is a little tricky but unpainted wood gives a much better adhesion.

15 Apply glue to the edge of the rail and the side of the stair support. Set the posts into place with the cut edge of the bottom cap flat to the side of the stair support. When removing the podiums, always hold the railings carefully at the podium edge. I stood a decorative plinth in front of these rails with a column base on top and a small beaded bouquet. You could, in theory, fit another square post at the podium side of the railing, cutting the railing a little shorter to accommodate it. However, I prefer not to have two identical posts next to each other.

16 Cut and fit a 4¼in (108mm) length of railing for the front of the podium, cutting off a small piece of the bottom rail which is to be next to the skirting to enable the handrail to fit flush against the wall. I kept this piece of railing in place with a decorative plinth on which I positioned another column base and a pineapple finial, and joined the two together with a little semi-permanent adhesive, again to allow for easy removal of the podium. Alternatively, remove a thin strip of carpet at the bottom front edge of the podium and glue the base of the railing to the podium itself. Repeat your chosen method at the other side.

Above right and right: Fill this floor with pretty hat displays and other beautiful accessories for the brides to peruse.

Part 3: The Attic Room

When creating such a large building, I usually make up the attic as a separate structure. You can then either set it into position permanently or, as I prefer, stand it on the top so that the building can be moved more easily. For the bridal salon it also means you can lay the upper floor chandelier wires underneath it quite safely rather than having to feed them up through the attic floor and base.

I have mainly decorated the attic in keeping with the rest of the salon. I wanted it to be a place where .the seamstress could receive clients for gown fittings and therefore thought it should be quite nicely decorated, too. Of course, how you choose to utilize this part of the salon is up to you. You could use part of it as a stockroom, for example, or perhaps as an extension of the main sales floors if you would like to add some further merchandise, such as a luggage display for the bridal trousseau. (Incidentally, the word 'trousseau' is derived from French word *trousse* meaning bundle, which referred to the bundle of clothes and possessions the bride carried to her new home.) There could be a small tea room in the attic, where customers can sit and discuss their purchases, or perhaps a wedding gift department. It's entirely your decision, simply do a little forward planning regarding the appropriate decoration and consider any extra or different components you may need to add to the list below. You can also make your attic deeper.

MATERIALS AND PREPARATION

Cut the following from ½in (12mm) MDF:

Ceiling and inner floor:

46in wide x 14in deep (1168 x 356mm)

Back:

11in high x 46in wide (279 x 1168mm)

Sides x 2:

12in high x 14in deep (305 x 356mm)

Dividing walls x 2:

11in high x 7in deep (279 x 178mm)

You will also need:

- ♥ *wooden cornice and skirting primed and painted; I have used Regency White*
- ♥ *wallpaper with any additional mouldings you may like to add, such as dado railing or picture rail in the tea shop*
- ♥ *carpet or floor covering*
- ♥ *five tulip wall lights*
- ♥ *11in (279mm) lengths of half round moulding with ½in (13mm) backs x 2, primed and painted in your chosen colour; I have used Regency White.*

1 Glue the back of the attic to the top of the floor surface flush with the back edge, and each side of the attic to the outside edge of the floor.

2 Glue the two lengths of half-round moulding to the front of the side walls to support the ceiling as you did at the front of the lower floor with the barley twist (see page 31). The edge of the moulding needs to be flush with the front edge of the wall.

3 Glue the two dividing walls into place using **O** as a guide to their position. These structures support the attic roof and need to be placed so that they are not in front of a window.

4 Lay the ceiling in place and draw around the dividing walls. Remove the ceiling and mask the areas you have drawn around as well as a further border in all the places where the cornice is to be fitted. Prime and paint the ceiling in your chosen colour. In keeping with the salon I have used Rose Pink.

5 Apply glue to the upper edges of the back and dividing walls, the top of the half-round mouldings and the side edges of the ceiling. Guide the ceiling into position and tape securely until dry to keep everything square. Always check the corners of rooms as they dry to make sure they don't slip from their 90-degree status.

6 Fit the three areas with cornice, lay flooring and apply your wallpaper and skirting with any further mouldings you may wish to add.

7 Drill and fit two wall lights to the two outer areas with a 6in (152mm) space on both sides of each. They need to be 9in (229mm) from the floor level. Install a fifth wall light to the centre of the middle area, also 9in (229mm) from the floor. Furnish according to the function of the room.

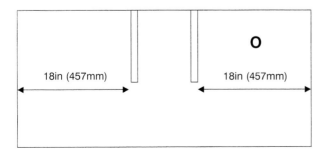

18in (457mm)   **O**   18in (457mm)

Part 4: The Façade

Main Façade

The main façade of a miniature building is the icing on the cake. The way to create an aesthetically pleasing façade is to find the correct balance between the necessary features and the fine details. Buildings with too many mouldings and trims can often look very fussy; as with most things, it's knowing when to stop. For the salon I wanted the windows to be the main focus and had them especially made, as well as the matching double door, to my own specifications. As the building is so large, I chose some fine details, such as the crown cornice, quoin stones and the plaster cameos.

MATERIALS AND PREPARATION

Cut from ⅜in (9mm) MDF:

Main façade:

42in high x 49in wide (1067 x 1245mm)

Cut from ¾in (18mm) MDF:

Step:

6½in wide x 3in deep (165 x 76mm)

You will also need:

♥ *5 large Palladian extended windows with a width of approximately 6½in (165mm) and a height of 10¼in (260mm)*

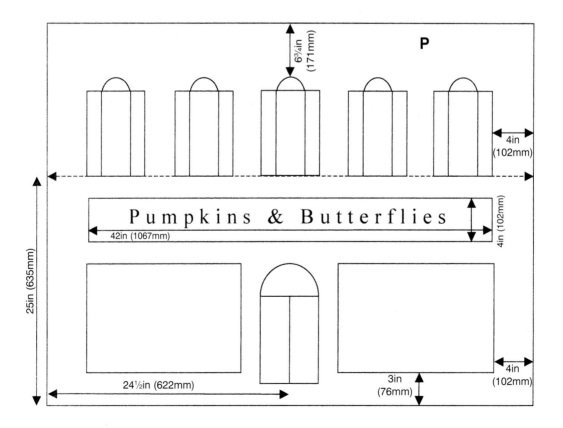

♥ *1 double Palladian door with an approximate height of 10¹/₂in (267mm) and width of 6in (152mm)*

♥ *2 main salon display windows approximately 9¹/₂in high x 12in wide (241 x 305mm) and 8 balcony supports*

♥ *1 board, 42 x 4in (1067 x 102mm), for the name sign, and 8ft (2.5m) of quadrant to frame it*

♥ *various optional plaster trims*

♥ *quoin stones*

♥ *optional crown cornice and corbels*

♥ *1 pair of hooks and eyes.*

1 Lay the façade on a flat surface. Find the centre at the bottom for positioning the door. With the step in place to find the correct placement for the door (but do not glue it on yet), draw around the inner door frame. Refer to diagram **P** on page 42 for the remaining window positioning.

2 Glue the balcony supports to the bottom of the two main display windows before placing them onto the façade 4in (102mm) in from the side and 3in (76mm) up from the bottom. Draw around them including the balcony supports, as these areas will need to be masked off for painting.

3 Measure 25in (635mm) up from the lower edge on both sides of the façade. Draw a line across for the placement of the windows. Place the first window directly above the door and the two outer windows 4in (102mm) in from the sides. Place the final two windows centrally between them.

4 Draw around the inner window frames then remove all the features to prime and paint along with the quoin stones, cornice and corbels.

5 Cut out the apertures then prime and paint the façade, masking off a narrow border down either side where the quoin stones are to be adhered, a border along the top where the crown cornice will be, the balcony supports and sign area. Remember to make the masked areas slightly smaller than the relevant feature to prevent gaps between them and the paintwork when they are applied.

6 Complete all remaining paintwork, apply trims, hooks and eyes and the name sign. Although I used to do signwriting many years ago, I am more than a little rusty and decided to treat myself to a professional touch. Hand-painted signs are, sadly, a dying art. The majority of sign makers now use PVC lettering but I much prefer the painted signs and you may have to look around if you prefer them too.

Attic Façade

I have constructed the attic façade with five windows. However, you could opt for a central door and extend a tearoom seating area or create a rooftop garden. The following is merely a guide to the details I chose.

MATERIALS AND PREPARATION
Cut from ⅜in (9mm) MDF:
> **Attic front:**
> 12in high x 47in wide (305 x 1194mm)

You will also need:
- ♥ *5 small Palladian attic windows with an approximate height of 7in (178mm) and a width of 4in (102mm)*
- ♥ *1 pair of hooks and eyes to keep the door in place at the top of the façade*
- ♥ *47in (1194mm) of quadrant.*

1 If using the same windows as I have, with a width of 4in (102mm), place them on the attic front with a 4½in (114mm) space between each one and the same space at each end, as illustrated in **Q**. For windows with an approximate height of 7in (178mm) they will need to be about 2½in (63mm) up from the bottom of the door, so draw this line on the attic front first.

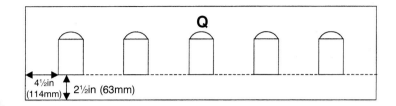

2 Carefully position the windows with the lower sill on the line. (Remember to draw around the back of the window and not the actual frame.) This is the size of the aperture you will need.

3 Cut out each hole for the windows following the guide to drilling outlined in Step 10 of the salon construction (page 22). If you have chosen different windows, remember to space them correctly and evenly so that the dividing walls of the attic are not on view behind them.

4 Prime and paint the front before gluing the painted windows into position. Paint and glue the quadrant along the top then fit the hooks and eyes.

Roof and Exterior

You can finish the roof in keeping with your chosen theme for the attic. You may just like to paint it or add moulded stone sheeting to the area in front of the attic. You could also add some baluster railings with small capped columns to the front two corners of the plinth.

1 Add a pediment to the centre of the top of the attic, using **R** as a guide.

2 I added some optional handrail to the upper edges of the pediment with a ¾in (19mm) square post at each side and a cap and pineapple finial to the top of them. I then added some plaster swags, tails and a central cherub.

3 Glue the pediment into place then paint the remainder of the attic roof and the outer sides of the salon.

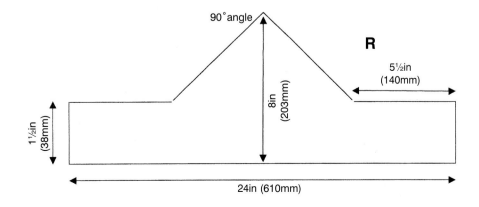

Salon Accessories Gallery

An illuminated display case is perfect for those special jewellery items.

Perfumes and toiletries for the bride.

Use decorative columns for small displays.

Create special displays with an arrangement of themed accessories.

With the salon complete, the fun part is filling it with miniature funishings and features, which are all important finishing touches.

A centrepiece provides a wonderful focal point.

Floral displays are an attractive addition.

Colour coordinate a small group of accessories.

Create displays of varied heights for maximum effect.

A Wedding Garden

MATERIALS AND PREPARATION

Cut from ⅜in (9mm) MDF:

Base:

24in wide x 23in deep (610 x 584mm)

Back:

5in high x 16½in wide (127 x 419mm)

Side:

5in high x 10in wide (127 x 254mm)

Cut from ¾in (18mm) MDF:

Upper level base:

18in wide x 11½in deep (457 x 292mm)

The best thing about making your own room box is that you can add to it as you wish and tailor it more easily to suit your own needs. This one makes a lovely setting for an outdoor reception or service.

You will also need:

- ♥ *8 trellis panels*
- ♥ *8 posts*
- ♥ *small rounded top and bottom rail and 4 balusters*
- ♥ *1 optional arch feature*
- ♥ *1 grass mat*
- ♥ *1 sheet of adhesive carpet cut in half lengthways*
- ♥ *1 sheet of stone wallpaper or moulded wall sheeting*
- ♥ *18in (457mm) length of ¹⁄₂in (13mm) stripwood*
- ♥ *18in (457mm) length of garden handrail x 2*
- ♥ *3 finials with base cap*
- ♥ *ready-made garden components from Anglesey Dolls' Houses (see page 188).*

1 Glue the upper level base to the left-hand corner of the garden base so that the side and back edges are flush.

2 Cut three 5¾in (146mm) lengths of ¾in (19mm) stripwood and glue one to the left-hand side of both the back and side walls so that the actual wall is half way between the edges of the stripwood. Glue the side wall at right angles to the back wall in the centre of the post (**A**).

3 Cut sufficient handrail for the two walls. You will need to join two pieces for the back wall. Cut the rail with a mitred join (**B**) and glue together on a flat, non-stick surface. Gently sand around the join on the upper three sides and glue into position on the walls with an even overhang.

4 Glue the third post to the right-hand side of the back wall before adding the finials.

5 Make up the small dividing feature. Glue the four balusters to the small rounded bottom rail and glue the second rail on top. Glue the structure at right angles and centrally to the left-hand side post on the side wall.

6 Glue together two posts and two trellis panels using **C** as a guide and six trellis panels and posts together using **D** as a guide.

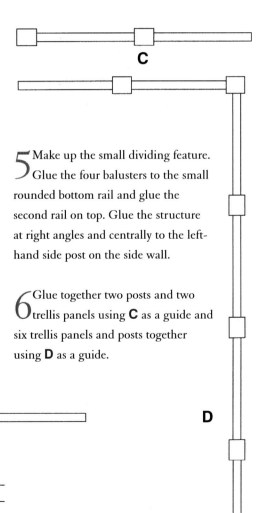

C

A

B

D

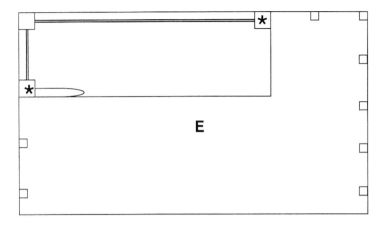

7 Paint the posts, dividing structure and the handrail on the walls, including the underside of the rail which overhangs the wall, and the two trellis and post structures. Leave a thin, unpainted area down each side of the end posts marked with a star (**E**) and the trellis which is going to be adhered to it. Apply the wall covering or moulded sheet to the two walls.

8 Using **E** as a guide, position all the structures on the garden base. Make sure that all the features are placed evenly and that the posts marked with a star meet the trellis before gluing everything into place. Now touch up any remaining bare unpainted areas where the trellis has been joined to the posts.

9 Position the carpet strip diagonally from the corner of the upper level. Take the carpet as far into the corner as possible. The flowers will cover the edge and neaten it up for you. Fold the carpet down the step and crease. Draw a line on both sides of the carpet on this upper level then remove it.

THE DOLLS' HOUSE WEDDING BOOK

10 Roughly estimate a piece of grass for the left-hand side of the carpet and cut. Place the grass up to the carpet line and from there into the wall side and fold. Cut down this fold line first, taking care not to go too far. Reposition the grass and carefully make further folds a little at a time until you have a perfect fit. Glue this piece of grass into position then repeat for the opposite side of the carpet on this upper level.

11 Apply wall covering to the riser of the step on each side of the carpet strip and the side of the upper level. You can peel back the adhesive cover strip of the carpet now and stick it into position on the upper level surface and the riser part of the step only. Do not remove the backing for the carpet which is to cover the lower level. This will ensure a good fit when fitting the remaining two pieces of grass.

12 Smooth the carpet down on the lower level and again draw a pencil line down each side. Now turn the carpet back and fit the remaining two grassy areas. Stick down the carpet and finish off.

The Flora

The plants you choose for your garden are entirely up to you. I have used quite a range of readily available plants in addition to work by fellow artisans and some of my own creations. The flower beds illustrated opposite are made quite easily with dried flower oasis. The three flower beds in the garden are corner beds.

1 First cut a 3½in (89mm) square cube of oasis from the corner of a block for the smaller corner beds and a 4in (102mm) square cube for the larger bed. Cut the cubes into 1in (25mm) thick slices.

2 Round the two opposite sides to the corner into a semi-circular shape and carefully shave the upper edge of the curved front of the flower bed into a gentle downward slope.

3 Mount the shape onto card and paint the upper surface of the oasis brown with acrylic paint and allow to dry overnight.

4 Now you are ready to plant your flowers. At the front I have planted some bush lobelia with slightly taller tiny handmade roses in an assortment of colours, some yucca leaves and small model railway gauge bushes behind them as centre fillers. Behind those I have placed some parchment roses, lavender sprigs, greenery sprays and flower spikes, and at the very back some porcelain climbing roses. I also made up a few urns in the same way (see left) with lavender sprigs at the back, a yucca plant in the centre, and some roses and tiny ivy sprigs at the front.

Sewing Creation

MATERIALS

♥ *Two small pieces of ³⁄₈in (9mm) MDF or similar thickness of plywood*

♥ *Paint*

♥ *Paper*

♥ *Carpet or flooring paper*

This cameo will appeal to those of you dedicated to sewing. It provides the perfect scene for a mannequin with a bridal gown in progress. A sewing machine, workbox with bobbins and stool complete the scene.

1 For the base, cut a rectangle 8in wide x 5in deep (203 x 127mm) and, using **A** as a guide, cut an arched back plate. A router will form a lovely finish to the upper curves of the back plate and the front edge and sides of the base. If this is not available, simply spend a little time rounding off these curves with a sanding block and finish with an extra-fine sandpaper sheet. Alternatively, glue some decorative moulding with mitred corners to the front and two side edges of the base.

2 Apply glue to the bottom edge of the back plate and glue it into place so that it is flush with the base at the back.

3 Finish the routed edges with paint and apply paper to the backplate.

4 Glue carpet or flooring paper to the base then accessorize as you wish.

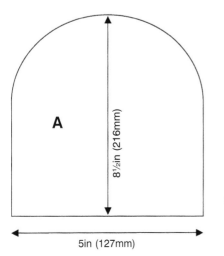

A

8½in (216mm)

5in (127mm)

Memories

Dedicated to the concept of 'granny's attic' this cameo has a walnut finish, a floral wall covering and plain carpet. Fill a trunk with items from yesteryear to recreate memories of a wedding that took place many years ago. You can use items found throughout the book including pretty lingerie, a bouquet, veil and headress. You could also add other items such as photographs in an album, a wedding certificate, keepsake box or a mannequin displaying the wedding gown.

To make this cameo, simply follow Steps 1–2 for Sewing Creation on the facing page then decorate and accessorize as you wish.

A further suggestion for a cameo is a 'Snapshot in Time', adding a model of your own or a friend's wedding gown and a dressed table, cake and menu.

Wedding Gowns

Anything is possible in the real world of wedding gown design, so why not try something a little less conventional in the miniature world? The gowns featured here are themed, as recent years have seen a rise in a themed approach to weddings. Particular design features or colours often permeate an entire wedding from the gown to the cake, bouquet, stationery and even the attire of the guests.

With these gowns I have used butterflies, paper leaves, roses, painted lace and minute arrowhead feathers in addition to a beautiful array of silks, laces, beads and crystals to create some really exciting designs.

I have also used striking colours for the gowns but for the more traditional bridal enthusiast, any of them can be created in white or ivory.

Fabrics and Equipment

Laces and Silks

I tend to be very selective when using lace for miniatures. An embroidered tulle is perhaps the most suitable for miniature bridal wear but it is important to choose an embroidery that is quite small and fine; some designs are just too heavy and large for miniatures.

You can create a small-scale shaped lace by carefully cutting around the pattern on a piece of tulle, such as the lace that has been trimmed for Royal Ascot (page 97), Ocean Dreams (page 113) and Hollywood Panache (page 104). This is the method used when trimming the hem of a full-size gown. A lace that has been applied straight with an upper line just doesn't look right unless it is on an historically influenced gown. You can add tiny crystals and beads to enhance the trimmed tulle,

either in a matching or contrasting shade to pick up the colour of a bouquet, for example. (Make sure you apply a fabric sealant such as Fray Check to the cut thread which links one part of the pattern to the next and trim the lace as close as possible to the pattern.)

Chantilly is a lovely soft lace but renowned for large patterns. I have found a very limited number of smaller patterns in this lace, the one used for Chantilly Mist (page 110) being an example. A lace of similar weight is French lace in gold or silver metallic; both have large patterns but you can use just part of the lace very effectively.

The most popular and versatile fabric for dressing miniatures is silk, the origin of which I find fascinating. According to Chinese legend,

silk was discovered almost 4,500 years ago when the young wife of Emperor Huang-Ti was sitting one day having tea under a mulberry tree. A silk cocoon dropped into her cup and she watched with amazement as the silky thread began to unravel in the hot liquid. Empress Si Ling Chi learned how to unwind the silk from a cocoon and weave it into fabric. It is said that this is how the silk industry began, and China still has the monopoly on silk production today.

Over the years, silk has become finer and smoother. It is durable yet luxuriously soft and it has the most beautiful sheen. The number of different kinds of silk in production today can sometimes lead to confusion, however. One thing to note is that some silks have a number after them. This is to do with the weight of the fabric. Generally, the higher the number, the heavier the silk.

Suitable Silks for Miniatures

Dupion is the most widely known silk popular for wedding gowns, Christening robes, embroidery, shoes and accessories, and it is the ultimate fabric for doll dressing. Available as a monotone fabric as well as a shot fabric (two colours of yarn used in the weave), there are some variations in quality to be aware of. Dupion can range from a slubby, slightly coarse weave to the finest Thai Princess silk which is a firm favourite of mine and I have used it extensively throughout the bridal designs. It has a lovely sheen as well as being so soft and semi-smooth. It is much easier to gather this finer silk fabric for those tiny waists, especially if you use a very small ¹⁄₁₆in (1–2mm) running stitch.

Silk Taffeta, sometimes called Supreme Silk, is a smooth, fine, crisp, plain-weave silk fabric with a lustrous finish. It can be pleated, pinched and draped quite effectively for miniatures but it is a little more expensive than Dupion.

Habutai, which is Chinese for 'soft as dawn' is a very lightweight and soft fabric with a good draping quality, although it cannot be shaped quite as effectively as Dupion and Taffeta. Most popular for silk painting, it is also used as a luxurious lining for full-size wedding gowns and suits.

Pongee is a lighter version of Habutai. It is sometimes known as China Silk and comes in different weights.

Indian Chiffon is a beautiful soft, sheer fabric with an excellent drape and fine crinkles. I find this perfect for miniature dressmaking.

Georgette is similar to chiffon but with an ultra-smooth finish. It is suitable for miniatures, but you will need to press folds and pleats to make them flatter and more natural in their appearance.

Organza is a smooth, stiff, sheer fabric, which can be plain, metallic, crinkled or shot. It does not drape or fold but makes excellent wings for miniature fairy costuming.

Mousselline is a sheer fabric like organza but much softer. Available in ribbon form, called Ruban Mousselline, it makes beautiful bows for tiny gowns.

Silk-backed Velvet is usually a viscose pile with a silk back.

Silk Jacquard and **Brocade** designs have a satinized raised pattern on a matte background. The back of the fabric has the design in reverse. On some costumes, both sides of the same fabric are utilized as part of the design.

Shantung, although a wild silk fabric, is quite fine with a definite visual weave or 'linen look'. It can be easily formed into soft folds and drapes for miniature dolls.

Silk Tulle has enabled me to explore and effectively create more gown styles than I ever thought possible. I couldn't believe the liquidity and fineness of this beautiful fabric when I first held it. I was even more surprised to find I could dye it, too, which was most useful as it was initially only available in three main colours: white, ivory and black. For those of you who are perhaps a little cautious about dyeing such an expensive fabric, I'm pleased to inform you that more colours of silk tulle, at the time of writing this book, are just becoming available and you will see some of them throughout the gown section. However, there is just one thing I'd like to point out. There are two forms of this tulle that I have encountered: a non-stretch and a stretch fabric. The non-stretch, available in white and ivory, is finer than the latter but a little stiffer and it frays quite badly. I would recommend this only for full-size veils that are to be edged. The stretch silk tulle, however, is perfect for miniatures. It is softer, does not fray, falls in beautiful drapes and is now available in a range of colours.

Equipment

There are a few sewing implements that I have found to be most useful in miniature dressmaking. The first of these is, without doubt, my miniature electric iron. This is a recent acquisition and I don't know how I managed to press those tiny seams without it. The sole plate, which is the same shape as a conventional household iron, measures only 1in (25mm) long and 1in (25mm) wide. If you use this together with a miniature ironing board, you will be surprised just how useful this is. Be warned though: although the irons are tiny, they do get hot! Miniature ironing board plans are available from me at the address given on page 188. Alternatively, there is a tool called a 'Mini Cut'n Press' initially used for patchwork but equally useful for miniature dressmaking. It consists of a 6in (152mm) square cutting mat with a printed grid for measuring and cutting and a printed padded reverse side for hemming and pressing.

Another tool I have found useful is not a sewing tool at all but something I created. I had one of those cake turntables used for icing and decorating cakes which was rapidly aging and losing its colour. I covered the top part of it with self-adhesive carpet and I use it to stand the dolls on as they are being dressed. As the final details are added to a gown, I can simply rotate the turntable and therefore minimize the handling of the gowns. It's brilliant!

Other sewing box 'must haves' include:

- ♥ *fine wedding and lace pins*
- ♥ *small quilting sewing needles*
- ♥ *beading sewing needles*
- ♥ *silk sewing thread*
- ♥ *tiny embroidery scissors*
- ♥ *dressmaking scissors*
- ♥ *dressmakers' awl*
- ♥ *tailors' chalk*
- ♥ *hem gauge*
- ♥ *seam ripper*
- ♥ *quilters' grid*
- ♥ *fabric sealant, such as Fray Check, and a small craft paintbrush for applying it*
- ♥ *a set of three tools for making tiny bows, rosettes and silk-ribbon roses*
- ♥ *rotary cutter and mat*

- ♥ *dressmakers' talc or similar fine powder for your hands when working with delicate fabric*
- ♥ *bent-nose tweezers for applying tiny pearls and paper leaves*
- ♥ *stationery 'pegs' – the type used for card-making are ideal for achieving a perfect bodice fit.*

On a final note I would like to recommend hair spray glitter mist, which is available in various colours, including gold and silver. If you spray it onto a finished tulle skirt or veil from a distance of about 1ft (30cm) whilst gently moving the spray in circular movements to prevent over-concentrating one area, it creates a 'sparkle tulle' in 1/12 scale. The glitter will hold well for gowns you are placing straight into a miniature scene.

The Basic Elements

Top Tips and Rules

1 The patterns have been created for slightly taller miniatures of 6in (152mm). This extra ½in (13mm) makes a real difference to the draping effect of long, flowing gowns. If you have a shorter doll, adjust the length of the skirt pattern only and for tiered tulle petticoats reduce the depth stated for each layer. For circular pattern pieces, such as Blue Moon (page 100), trim ¼in (6mm) from the entire outline.

2 Always paint the shoes on the feet of a doll before fitting the dress (see page 148 for guidance on painting shoes).

3 Always sew a ⅛in (3mm) seam, unless an alternative is stated, and about a ¹⁄₁₆in (1.5mm) hem for skirts with a curved hemline.

4 Sew short seams on bodices and corsets by hand with a tiny, even running stitch or backstitch and longer seams on full skirts either by hand or with a short machine stitch.

5 Make your running stitches as small as possible – about ¹⁄₁₆in (1.5mm). This will require a little practice but it is worthwhile.

6 Cut pattern pieces on the bias. To do this, line up the arrows parallel with the selvedge of the fabric and at right angles to the visible grain of the fabric.

7 Always apply Fray Check fabric sealant to pattern pieces. Use a fine paintbrush and lay the fabric on some white kitchen towel. Pour the Fray Check into a small plastic dish a little at a time. Wash the brush immediately with warm water and a little detergent. You will see that any Fray Check still on the brush will turn white. Remove this gently with a pin.

8 When cutting silk tulle with a rotary cutter on a cutting mat, don't press too hard as you may force the fabric into a groove and it could ladder as you try to remove it. Instead, gently tease the tulle from the mat and use sharp scissors to cut any threads the cutter may have missed. Cut the tulle with a new blade and use this blade only when cutting silk tulle.

9 When making tiny sleeves, especially narrow fitting sleeves, first sew the underarm seam. Then, instead of fastening off the thread, pass the needle down the sleeve and gently pull the thread which will roll the sleeve through to the right side.

10 If you prick your finger whilst sewing on silk, take the sewing straight to the tap and apply cold water with the fingertip until the stain disappears. Don't overwet the fabric. Lay the silk on a towel and apply pressure with white kitchen roll to remove all the moisture.

ℳetticoats

Just as full-size gowns require the correct
undergarment, miniatures also need appropriate
support if a gown is going to sit right. When
dressing miniatures, petticoats should really have
a utilitarian function rather than being purely
decorative. A petticoat without purpose will just
add unnecessary bulk. I would use a petticoat,
therefore, for two reasons only: if the fabric the
main outfit is made from is either sheer or semi-
sheer, or if a gown requires some definite form of
support. The latter function of the petticoat is the
one which we need to explore in more detail and
the following instructions for a range of support
petticoats and additions will be cross-referenced
and referred to in the gown sections for the
relevant designs.

Petticoat 1: Basic Straight Style
for Sheer Gowns

This petticoat serves the purpose of a conventional
underskirt to line a semi-sheer or sheer gown made
from, for example, chiffon or georgette. You need
this petticoat to be quite slim fitting, as it must not
alter the shape of the dress or add bulk to the waist.

To make a simple version of this petticoat:

1 Cut out the one-piece skirt using the pattern
provided on page 164.

2 Fold the fabric in half down the centre front
and mark with a pin.

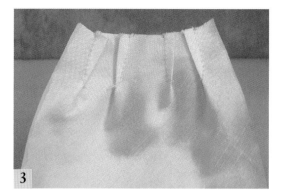

3 Fold in and sew the two tiny darts at each side
of the petticoat front and one on each side of
the open back edges.

4 Press the two darts on each side of the centre
front towards each other.

5 Sew a neat back seam starting at the bottom of
the petticoat and stop in plenty of time to fit
the petticoat to the doll but do not fasten off.

6 Press the seam open and fit onto the doll before
closing the seam.

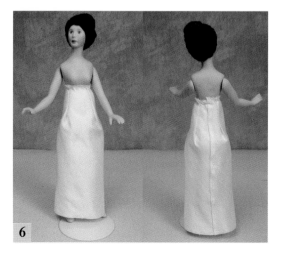

Petticoat 2: The Simple 'Add On'

This petticoat is an extension of the previous style.

1 Make up Petticoat 1 and add either a 1–2in (25–51mm) layer of silk tulle around the hemline for a little extra fullness or a gathered piece of polyester tulle at the back, forming a bustle-style support. The latter option should be formed by cutting a rectangle of tulle that is approximately 4–5in (102–127mm) wide and the length required for the gown (it should reach the hemline of the gown or train).

2 Round off the outer corners, as for the basic drape veil (see pages 126–127) and gather the upper edge before sewing it into position at the back of the doll. Finish with a bow.

3 Alternatively, you can attach a tulle 'add on' to the fabric part of the doll's body without the petticoat if you require only a little support at the back.

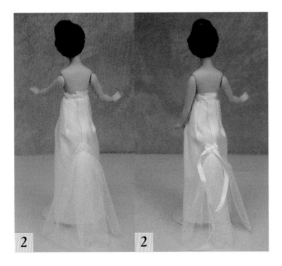

Petticoat 3: Silk Tulle Underskirt and Skirt

The first and second tiers of this petticoat, followed with a third or even fourth top layer, actually form both the petticoat and the gown, as shown in the 'Little Sew' gown (page 78), 'Rose Garden' (page 81) and 'Pumpkins and Butterflies' (page 117). This process requires accuracy when cutting the tulle strips. Simply use three or four strips of tulle, the width of the fabric applied to the doll or mannequin one just above the other. This cuts the bulk around the waist seam; otherwise it would be too heavy for the stitches to hold.

Petticoat 4: The Advanced 'Add On' and 'Shaper'

As the name suggests, this is the ultimate engineered petticoat; it plays a significant role in the overall shape of a gown or costume. This petticoat can require a combination of the former three petticoat styles as well as shaping the various layers so that they provide a firm foundation for the gown. The 'Swan Lake' design on page 87, for example, has three parts to the petticoat:

1 The first layer is a straight 60in (1524mm) strip of silk tulle 3½in (89mm) deep, which has been gathered at the top and attached to the doll so that the bottom of the petticoat is at floor level.

2 The second strip of silk tulle is 4¼in (108mm) deep and, after gathering the upper edge, is attached to the doll just above the first at the front and sides, again so that it rests upon the floor. At the back, however, the two ends of the tulle are dipped so that the support is taken away from the waist where it needs to be flat and added to the lower back where the train begins. ¼in (7mm) silk ribbon is used to tidy up the top edges.

3

3 A third piece of polyester tulle has then been cut, this time as for the simple 'add on', and attached to the base of the dipped former layer as in Step 2 for Petticoat 2.

By building up the layers and separate additions in this way, you can create beautifully shaped gowns. It does take a little practice but all you need to do is think carefully about the shape of the gown you are making and which parts need support then proceed to supply the support – that is basically all you have to remember.

1 2

Bodices

There are two basic bodices, elements of which I have combined and used for the gowns throughout this book. In the instructions for each gown, it clearly states which combination of bodice pieces you will need from the following options, unless an alternative is offered.

Note

You will need to apply iron-on ultra-light interfacing to the fabric before cutting out the bodice pattern pieces and apply Fray Check fabric sealant to all edges. Tips are included to help you achieve a better fit for a specific doll or mannequin of your own choice.

Bodice Patterns

My preferred choice of bodice is the five-part bodice. It is a little tricky and you will need to practise as I did, but it does offer the best fit. Patterns for the bodices are on pages 164–165.

Bodice A has:

- ♥ short sides
- ♥ dipped lower back
- ♥ 'v' shaped or 'dipped' lower front
- ♥ straight or sweetheart neckline.

Bodice B has:

- ♥ medium-length sides
- ♥ dipped lower back
- ♥ 'v' shaped or 'dipped' lower front
- ♥ straight or sweetheart neckline.

Cutting and Layout of Pattern Pieces

When cutting out two bodice parts that are to be opposite one another, such as the two sides, the instructions state to cut one side in reverse. This means you fold the fabric selvedge to selvedge after ironing on the interfacing and lay the pattern pieces on the bias so that the arrow lines are parallel with the selvedge (**1**). To cut a single pattern piece on the bias where there is a central fold, such as with some of the skirt fronts, fold the fabric diagonally (**2**) and place the central fold of the skirt on the diagonal fold.

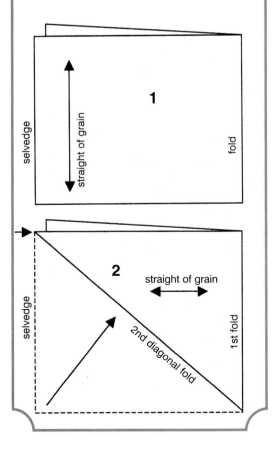

Adapting the Bodice Patterns

Different dolls and mannequins do vary slightly in shape if not in size. To create the best fit for your doll or mannequin, first make up a basic bodice front and sides with tacking stitch following steps 1 and 2 below and fit it onto your doll or mannequin to check the size. The side edges need to be just past the underarm line towards the back of the doll to allow for a small seam. Adapt the pattern if necessary by noting where this part of the bodice is either too big or too small. Mark the changes you have to make on the relevant pattern pieces. It may be a case of trial and error until you achieve the best fit. Add the back pieces (Step 3) to either the first front and sides you made or an adapted front and sides you have created from the modified first. Make up the rest of your practice bodice as instructed in Steps 4 and 5.

If you are new to the hobby you may find it helpful to make one or two preliminary bodices before creating one for your chosen gown. Become familiar with the pressing of seams and the snipping of curves, the shape of the lower edge and the bust shaping which often requires little more than some shaping with the fingertips after sewing to achieve the desired shape. Cutting silk on the bias enables you to easily form and shape part of a garment in this way.

Fit the bodice onto the doll or mannequin and again gently work the fabric around the doll's shape for a perfect fit. A well-fitted bodice is crucial to the appearance of the finished gown so it is worth spending a little time achieving the best fit you possibly can. You will probably be surprised at how effectively the silk bodice retains its shape when you remove it from the doll.

Making Up the Bodice:

1 Sew a tiny running stitch down the bodice sides as indicated with a dotted line on the pattern piece (see page 164).

2 Pull the edge of the first side and gently ease it as you pin it with right sides together to the corresponding side on the bodice front and sew a $\frac{1}{8}$in (3mm) seam. Repeat for the second side.

3 Join the two back pieces to the sides in turn and press the seams open. Work the sides gently with your fingertips so that they curve outwards when turned through to the right side.

4 Fit the bodice around the doll. You can join the back seam in two ways, neither of which is to be worked yet but you do need to fit and press at this stage. The first involves drawing the two sides together by oversewing them using minute stitches. This will give you a seam that is in the exact centre of the back. This method is ideal for button-backed gowns and those with large embellishments or ornate tails. Draw the two sides of the back together using a few little stationery pegs to achieve the perfect fit. Pin where the back edges must be folded under so that they both meet edge to edge down the centre of the back. Remove the bodice and press the back edges under.

5 The second is a neatly glued and concealed centre back when you don't want to see an obvious join, which in real life would apply to zipped gowns and those with shawl collars. In this instance you need to turn under the left-hand side of the back as you look at it so that it can be glued onto the straight and flat right-hand side so that the overlapped edge is down the centre of the back. Now remove the bodice and press the turned under edge.

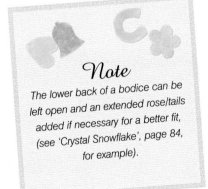

6

6 Apply one spot of PVA glue to the top and bottom of each side of the four seams to keep them flat and neat at these points. Starting at the lower edge on one side of the 'v', fold under, press and glue a ⅛in (3mm) hem along the first side of the lower edge of the bodice right along the back edge. Return to the other side of the 'v' and repeat the process, making sure that the actual 'v' is neatly folded and glued. Turn under and glue a ⅛in (3mm) hem along the entire upper edge of the straight top bodice front. Press before pinning into place on the doll and securing it in the relevant way.

7 For a rounded dipped front, turn under the rounded part first at the centre front and for a shaped top form the two 'v's as you did for the previous bodice's lower edge, making a tiny snip in the centre of the 'v's to allow them to lie flat.

Trains

There are two basic gown trains, which I have included in some of the designs. The train that is part of the skirt and therefore defines the form and shape of the skirt is the Integral Train. Examples of this can be seen on Chantilly Mist (page 110) and Swan Lake (page 87). The second is the detachable train which, when making miniatures, is more of

an 'add on' rather than a 'take off'. I've included it simply as an alternative design and one that is easier to achieve if you are making your first wedding gown. This form of train can be seen on Royal Ascot (below). Integral trains can be extended further with shaped 'add ons' (see Swan Lake, left), and a tulle drape (see Chantilly Mist, bottom left).

There are six lengths of integral train. The first is the Sweep, which extends to the bottom of a miniature gown by about 1in (25mm). The second is the Court, which extends by about 1½in (38mm). The third is the Chapel, which extends 5in (127mm) from the waistline. The fourth is the Semi Cathedral, seen on 'Swan Lake' (above left). It extends by 6½in (165mm) from the waistline. The fifth is the Cathedral, which extends by 7½–8in (190–203mm) and seen on Chantilly Mist (far left). The longest is the Royal Cathedral or Monarch, which extends from 9in (230mm) plus.

Embellishments

Roses

There are basically three forms of rose that can be added to the miniature gown. The first is the silk ribbon rose. These can range in size from ⅛in (3mm) using ¹⁄₁₆in (2mm) silk ribbon to ½in (13mm) in diameter using ³⁄₁₆in (4mm) silk ribbon. The smaller roses are perfect for necklines, headdresses, hats, flower baskets, and the such like, while the larger ones are dramatic and make a statement on *Cinderella*-style skirts, the back of waists or the front side of a gown.

A larger bloom also makes a stunning headdress when teamed with a feather such as the one used for the 'A Taste of Honey' gown (page 107). These larger blooms can either be self-coloured or variegated like the roses in the 'Rose Garden' gown (page 81). You can also use three shades of ribbon with the deeper colour in the centre, a slightly lighter shade next then a very pale shade on the outside of the rose, each colour being glued firmly down before starting the next.

Silk Ribbon Rose Sizes

Tiny Made with ¹⁄₁₆in (2mm) silk ribbon. Approximate diameter of ⅛in (3mm)

Small Made with ¹⁄₁₆in (2mm) or ³⁄₁₆in (4mm) silk ribbon. Approximate diameter of ³⁄₁₆in (4mm).

Medium Made with ³⁄₁₆in (4mm) silk ribbon. Approximate diameter of ¼in (6mm).

Large Made with ³⁄₁₆in (4mm) silk ribbon. Approximate diameter of ⅜in (10mm).

Extended Made with ³⁄₁₆in (4mm) silk ribbon. Approximate diameter of ½in (12mm).

To Make a Large Bloom:

1 First begin your rose on a rose maker with one or two wraps around the tool. Fold the ribbon diagonally to the back and place a dot at the base of the rose on the rose maker. These form the petals.

2 Repeat this process making a quarter turn at a time, as shown on the right.

3 Eventually, instead of placing a dot at the base of the maker, you will be gluing the edge of the diagonally folded ribbon to the underside of the larger rose.

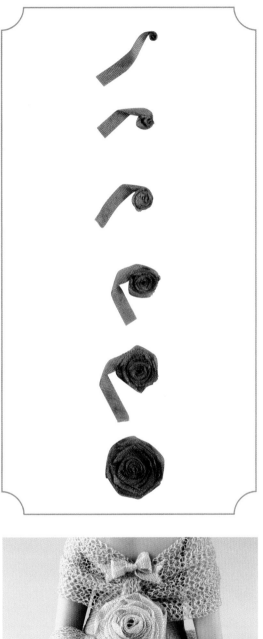

The second rose is made from silk fabric (see picture at bottom of page 70). They are made from the same silk or a coordinating colour fabric to the dress.

To Make a Silk Fabric Rose:

1 First cut out the pattern piece on page 165 on the bias.

2 Apply Fray Check fabric sealant to the entire edge, fold in half and sew a row of tiny gathering stitches along the entire curved edge.

3 Pull this gathering row very gently and begin twirling the rose, fixing it with a small stitch or a spot of glue as you proceed.

The third type of rose is far easier to obtain. These are the miniature parchment and fabric roses, as shown on the 'Little Sew' headdress (page 78), which can be bought ready made.

Rose Leaves

You can make small leaves for your roses in two ways. A small piece of $\frac{1}{16}$in (2mm) ribbon, looped in a figure eight is perfect for tiny roses but you can make larger leaves by sandwiching two layers of organza together with some double-sided interfacing and manually cutting leaf shapes. Use a range of colours for your leaves and even a combination of fabric and paper leaves for maximum effect.

Bows

I prefer a simple bow for the back of gowns, as large bows tend to overpower miniatures. I usually use a bow maker, such as the one shown below, as these provide such even and neat results. A $\frac{3}{8}$in (10mm) or $\frac{5}{8}$in (15mm) Ruban Mousseline ribbon is my favourite material.

To Make a Large Bow:

1 Fold a 3in (76mm) length of ¾in (20mm) ribbon in half and mark the centre by gently pinching it.

2 Join the edges with a small seam and press the seam open and turn through to the right side.

3 Place the pinched centre of the ribbon on the back seam and run a row of tiny gathering stitches down the centre.

4 Pull the gathers and use a ¹⁄₁₆in (2mm) or ³⁄₁₆in (4mm) ribbon in the same shade to form a knot around the centre of the bow. Make two tails from the ribbon, cutting a 'v' in the end and apply Fray Check fabric sealant to the cut edges.

5 The centre of the bows can then be decorated with crystals, beads or silk roses as shown left on Royal Ascot.

To Make a Fabric Bow:

1 Cut a piece of silk 2 x 1in (51 x 25mm) and apply Fray Check fabric sealant to all edges.

2 Turn under and press a ¹⁄₈in (3mm) hem on all sides, cutting a tiny triangle off the corners. Now use the slightest dot of glue to hold the hems down.

3 Gather the centre of the fabric as for the large bow instructions above.

4 Gently pull the two sides of the bow downwards to give the effect of a heavy bow. then place a small rose on the gathered centre.

Drapes and Tails

Instead of making simple tails from ribbon, you can add some more dramatic tails and small drapes to the base of a pretty bow, rose, or a combination of the two. I have included pattern pieces for some shaped tails and two sizes of drape (see page 165). You can experiment with additional sizes and gradients of drape using these as a starting point.

1 Turn under and glue a ¹⁄₈in (3mm) hem on the lower three sides of each shape and on all sides of the folded centre tails.

2 Sew a row of stitches as indicated on the pattern pieces and gather gently before fastening off the thread.

3 Position the drapes or tails on the gown and finish with a bow, roses or indeed something a little bit different…

Something a Bit Different...

This is where you can be unconventional and really have some fun. On the 'Pumpkins and Butterflies' gown (below right) I added tiny butterflies and a larger organza butterfly using the same principle as the leaves for the roses (see page 72). To the 'Rose Garden' gown (right) I added some pretty ivy sprigs, and to 'Ocean Dreams' (below) I applied sea shells. Further ideas include a champagne and strawberry theme with miniature polymer clay strawberries cascading down the back of a champagne-coloured silk gown; tiny sequin dust stars could also be scattered on the back of a gown or perhaps some trailing 'babies' breath'. The possibilities are endless – just let your imagination flow!

Quick and Easy Gowns

♥ Complete Beginner

No Sew

This is by far the easiest gown you will ever create. I've only used this design on miniature mannequins for shop and room settings but see no reason why it could not be adapted for a miniature doll as well.

MATERIALS
♥ *Narrow lace*
♥ *12 x 6in (305 x 152mm) piece of silk*
♥ *A mannequin or hard-bodied doll*
♥ *Double-sided sticky tape*
♥ *PVA*
♥ *A tiny pleater*

1 Apply some double-sided tape around the bust line of the mannequin and then in strips around the remainder of the body.

2 Fold over ¼in (6mm) on one long side of the silk, keep in position with a few dots of PVA then press. Apply the centre of that folded edge to the centre of the mannequin's bust. At the back of the mannequin, pinch the two sides of the fabric together tightly at the waist to ensure a snug fit and sew a couple of stitches to hold it in place.

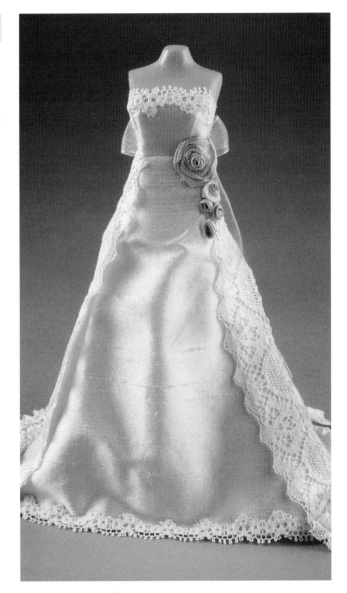

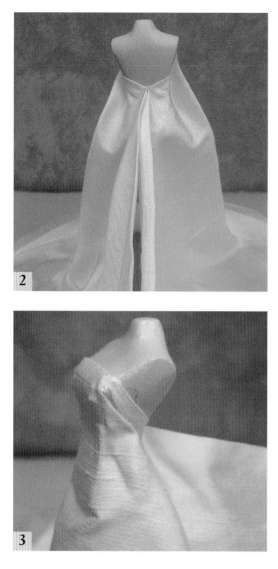

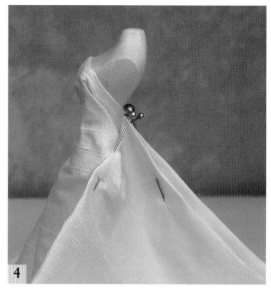

4 At the back of the mannequin, form gentle folds to disguise the centre back of the train, which you can pin together for the moment. At the front, bring the two sides of the skirt train round and pin into position. Adjust the back seam of the train so that it hangs correctly.

5 Trim the front hem of the skirt to floor level and the two sides of the train so that they just sweep the floor. Apply Fray Check fabric sealant to the entire hemline and leave to dry.

3 At the front of the mannequin, pleat the fabric at each side of the bodice front where a real dress would have darts for shaping. Take these pleats backwards and glue them down flat against the side of the mannequin. Smooth the fabric over the taped areas until they are nice and smooth.

6 Press the fold at the centre back seam of the mannequin and apply a little glue to keep it in place.

7 Glue some flat or pleated lace to the hemline of the gown and some flat lace to the front edges of the train. You could also put a little lace around the top of the bodice. Add some optional silk roses to the side waist of the gown and to the back of the waist where the train has been pinched together. Alternatively, add a pretty bow to this area.

Little Sew

This is another easy style to make yet ever so pretty. The gown is a little longer than ballet length, as this is a simpler measurement to cut and position. If you would prefer a full-length tulle tiered gown then follow the measurements and instructions for the three tulle layers of the 'Rose Garden' gown (page 82) before adding the simple lace bodice. All this style requires are running stitch gathers along the top edges of the three tulle skirt tiers and a particular lace with an edge that can simulate a 'Sweetheart' neckline. I complemented the gown with a lace tiara and a cathedral-length basic drape-styled veil. Some tiny parchment roses completed the ensemble.

MATERIALS

♥ *Three strips of tulle, each the full width of the fabric (or 60in/1524mm) 3¹⁄₂in (89mm), 4in (102mm) and 4¹⁄₂in (114mm) deep*

♥ *One rectangle of tulle for the veil 9in wide x 10in long (229 x 254mm)*

♥ *A small piece of gold lace*

♥ *Gold Ruban Mousseline bow made from ³⁄₈in (10mm) ribbon*

♥ *A small piece of ¹⁄₃₂in (0.6mm) craft wire for the tiara base*

♥ *2 large and 2 small parchment roses*

♥ *Optional glitter mist hair spray*

1 Gather the upper long edge on each of the three tulle strips. Always go up and come down a hole in the tulle and not the yarn, which can damage the delicate tulle.

2 Pull up the gathers on the shortest tier and evenly pin it around the waist of your doll so that the lower edge is resting on the ankle and the open edge is at the centre back. Attach the 4in (102mm) tier in the same way with the sewing line just above the previous tier. Finally add the 4½in (114mm) tier.

3 Cut the lace as shown below. I have cut a ½in (13mm) piece for below the waist so that the front has a dip. The upper part needs to fit your doll from the shoulders to the waist. You will need to cut out a space for the arms where there is no embroidery and make a tiny cut where a normal gown would have darts on each side of the bodice front. Apply Fray Check fabric sealant to all the cut edges of the lace, especially where you have cut the embroidery threads. The doll will need a lining for the lace bodice made with a simple band of wide silk ribbon around the bust line.

4

4 Fit the lower part of the lace around the waist of the doll, as shown here on a doll with a plain petticoat for a clearer view, and glue into position at the back with a little PVA. Attach the upper part of the bodice, applying glue to the waist band, snipped 'darts' and the back edge.

5 Fold the tulle veil in half lengthways so that the longest side is the length then round off the outer corners. Gather the upper edge tightly and attach to the base of the hair.

6 Cut a ½in (13mm) curved piece of lace with a height of approximately ³⁄₁₆in (5mm) and apply Fray Check immediately. Bend the piece of craft wire around a tubular shape with a ½in (13mm) diameter and cut so that it fits the front of the doll's hair. Glue the lace to the centre of the wire and then add a large rose (see page 71). Glue one large and two smaller buds to the waist of the gown and the gold Ruban Mousseline bow to the back. Finish the tulle skirt with a dusting of spray glitter mist.

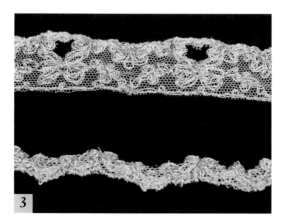

3

Themed Gowns

Rose Garden

♥ ♥ Simple

MATERIALS

- ♥ *14in (357mm) of 69in (1750mm) wide ivory silk tulle for the three skirt layers*
- ♥ *Small quantity of deep gold lace with a lower central scallop for the apron base*
- ♥ *Small quantity of all-over gold lace for the bodice centre front*
- ♥ *4¼ x 1in (108 x 25mm) gold lace for the apron sides*
- ♥ *Metallic gold Perle embroidery floss for faux piping on the bodice front*
- ♥ *Ivy trails and some individual gold ivy leaves*
- ♥ *6 gold birch leaves for the lower edges of the lace stitched onto the sides of the gold apron*
- ♥ *³⁄₁₆in (4mm) pink 'flamingo' variegated ribbon or three shades of ³⁄₁₆in (4mm) pink silk ribbon to create roses with a dark centre graduating out to paler outer petals (see pages 70–71)*
- ♥ *pink organza bow, approximately ³⁄₈in (10mm), for the back of the gown*
- ♥ *¼in (6mm) narrow ivory lace, pre-pleated to a finished length to fit around the lower edge of the bodice (remember to apply Fray Check fabric sealant to upper edge if cutting the trim from a wider lace and always cut above a pattern line)*
- ♥ *Ivory silk for the bodice*

Over a tiered ivory silk tulle underskirt, a myriad of variegated pink roses and gold highlighted ivy rest against a gold apron and over the shoulder of a gold highlighted bodice with a frilled lower edge. A ribbon choker with a rose and a single rose in her hair completes the wedding outfit.

1 Each layer of tulle is the full width of the fabric. Cut the first layer 3½in (89mm) deep and sew a gathering line along the top edge. Fit and pin around your doll so that the tulle rests perfectly on the floor, easing the gathers evenly around the figure. Sew into place.

2 Cut a second layer 4¼in (108mm) deep and gather as for the first strip. Pin and stitch just above the first layer, again so that the tulle rests on the floor.

3 Cut a top layer 5in (127mm) deep and repeat the gathering, pinning and stitching stage. This completes the tulle tiered skirt.

4 Cut a gold lace apron base 4¼in (108mm) long with a 1in (25mm) top and tapering out to a 2¼in (57mm) bottom with a central scallop. Stitch 1in (25mm) lace down the two side edges so that the lace is back to back at the top and slightly apart at the bottom. Glue the birch leaves across the two lower edges of this lace.

5 Glue three ivy trails with gold ivy leaf highlights down the front of the apron together with an arrangement of medium, large and extended silk ribbon roses (see pages 70–71) as shown in the photograph. Now stitch the apron into position.

6 Make up Bodice A with a dipped lower front and back and a sweetheart neckline (see pages 66–68), but add a gold lace centre front, cut using the same pattern, and place it together with the silk centre front. Add the faux piping to the seams and a frilled lower edge.

7 Fit the bodice onto the doll with a trail of ivy over the right shoulder, a medium silk rose at the side waist and the organza bow and another extended rose at the back waist.

Crystal Snowflake

♥ ♥ Simple

This fairytale gown is in purest white silk and has a sprinkling of Swarovski crystal dust. Silver maple leaves provide the perfect finishing touch.

MATERIALS

- ♥ *120 x 3¹/₂in (3m x 89mm) strip of white soft-quality polyester tulle for the petticoat*
- ♥ *14in (356mm) square of white silk for the overskirt*
- ♥ *Silver metallic silk for the underskirt*
- ♥ *Swarovski crystals (optional)*
- ♥ *Large quantity of silver maple paper leaves sprayed with a paper gloss for reinforcement*
- ♥ *One extended white silk rose (see pages 70–71)*
- ♥ *Small quantity of ³/₈in (10mm) silver organza ribbon and ¹/₄in (7mm) white silk ribbon*
- ♥ *Patterns on pages 166–167*

1 Sew a row of gathering stitches ¹/₈in (3mm) down from the upper edge of the polyester tulle. This can be worked by machine. Sew another row ¹/₄in (6mm) down from the first line of stitches and a third row ¹/₄in (6mm) down from this one. Pull the gathers to fit snugly around the doll and fasten off the threads. Lay this tulle overnight under a very heavy weight.

2 Wrap the tulle petticoat around the doll and secure at the waist. Sew a row of stitches ¼in (6mm) down from the waist through the soft body of the doll. Sew another row just beneath it. This form of underskirt will support a silk skirt but it is essential to keep the gathers firm. If it is spreading out too much, sew a row of stitches through the most bulky part until you have sculpted the correct shape you need.

3 Cut and apply Fray Check fabric sealant to the silver tulle underskirt. Place at the waist, slightly offset towards the right-hand side.

4 Cut out the white silk overskirt, Fray Check all the edges and sew a row of gathering stitches ⅛in (3mm) down from the upper edge. Pull the threads and fit around the doll with the open side over the silver insert.

5 Make up Bodice A with 'v' lower front and back and straight neckline (see pages 66–68). Apply a thin layer of glue across the neckline of the bodice and add some optional crystals. Add a few silver maple leaves to the inside edge of the neckline with the pointed edges facing upwards. Fit the bodice onto the doll and secure.

6 Glue a row of silver maple leaves around the entire hem of the overskirt with a dusting of optional crystals. Attach two silver organza ribbon tails (see page 73) with diagonal tips to the overlap at the side front waist and glue a circle of silver maple leaves around the edge of the rose before gluing it over the top of the tails. Attach a ¼in (7mm) white silk bow to the back waist.

Swan Lake

♥ ♥ ♥ Experienced

MATERIALS

- ♥ *Pale pink silk for the bodice and gown*
- ♥ *¹/₁₆in (2mm), ³/₁₆in (4mm) and ¹/₄in (7mm) baby pink silk ribbons for the tiny bows and roses*
- ♥ *Small piece of 5¹/₂in (140mm) pink decorative tulle to support the train*
- ♥ *3 pearly pink paper water lilies and a few extra petals*
- ♥ *1 white marabou feather*
- ♥ *Patterns on pages 168–169*

A pink silk gown with elongated fitted graceful waist and hip and beautifully shaped skirt provides the background for some pretty bows and waterlilies. I painted her shoes pink and added two tiny ¹/₁₆in (2mm) silk ribbon bows. Her headdress was created with a single water lily and I curled ten strands of marabou, each only 1–1¹/₂in (25–38mm) long after gluing the bottom ends together. Curl the feathers in the same way as you would gift ribbon, holding them tightly and running the edge of a pair of scissors underneath them.

1 Prepare the doll with Petticoat 4 (see page 65) but don't position the 'add on' piece until the skirt is fitted.

2 Make up the five-piece skirt turning under the hem and stitching a row of gathers ¹/₈in (3mm) down from the upper edge. Fit the skirt onto the doll and pull the gathers gently and evenly around the waist then fasten off.

3 Cut a tulle 'add on', as described in Petticoat 2 (see page 64), to support the train. Pin this to the petticoat, so that the edge of the tulle reaches the hem of the skirt, and then secure with a few stitches.

4 Turn under a ⅛in (3mm) hem all around the train apart from the upper edge, snipping the lower curve and gluing the tabs down into position with a little glue. Gather the upper edge, pulling the thread until the gathers are ⅝in (15mm) wide. Glue the train into place so that the lower edge protrudes from the hem of the dress by ½–¾in (13–19mm), according to taste.

5 Make up Bodice A with dipped lower back, 'v' shaped lower front and straight neckline (see pages 66–68). Fit and secure into position.

6 Add to the gathers of the train an extended silk ribbon rose made with a ¼in (7mm) silk ribbon which has 4in (102mm) tails just below it and a water lily on top of the knot of the bow. Attach a medium silk rose to each side of the extended rose and one below the water lily with a few pearly water lily leaves underneath them so that the ends protrude slightly (see pages 70–73 for information on roses, tails and bows).

7 To the back of the waist, add a ¼in (7mm) silk bow with ½in (13mm) tails.

8 Finally, on the bodice front add a ¼in (7mm) bow with no tails, made from ³⁄₁₆in (4mm) silk ribbon, just below the bust line and then a second water lily to the right-hand side of the straight neckline.

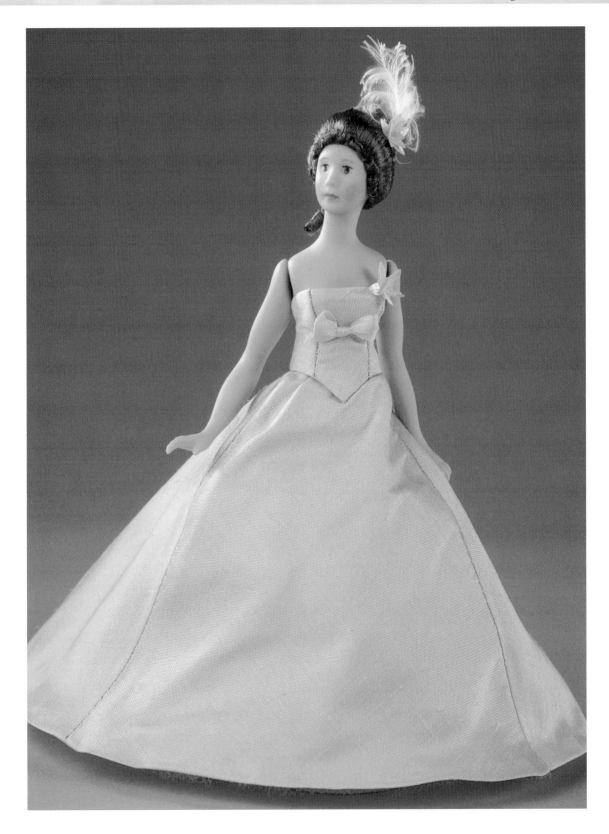

La Dolce Vita

MATERIALS

- ♥ *12in (305mm) square of antique gold silk for the fitted skirt*
- ♥ *12in (305mm) of 69in (1750mm) wide gold silk tulle for the train*
- ♥ *5 x 3½in (127 x 89mm) piece of gold silk tulle for the shawl collar*
- ♥ *³⁄₁₆in (4mm) ecru silk ribbon*
- ♥ *Gold glitter mist hair spray*
- ♥ *Patterns on page 170*

This indulgent design is inspired by that famous Italian term meaning 'The Good Life'. It is made from antique gold silk and has a draped fitted skirt plus a multi-layered gold silk tulle train. I painted her shoes to match the gown using Winsor and Newton old gold acrylic paint and added two tiny shoe bows using beige ³⁄₁₆in (4mm) ecru silk ribbon and a bow maker. You can add a little gold glitter to the painted toe of the shoe if you wish, or even cover the entire shoe 'upper' for a very glitzy look.

1 Make a short fold in the skirt fabric, as indicated on the pattern piece on page 170 and marked with Star 2. Take this fold up and place it on top of Star 1. Make another fold at Star 3 and place this on Star 2, so that the pleat itself is just ¹⁄₁₆in (about 1mm) below the first pleat. This is the right side of the skirt. Pin then repeat for the opposite side.

2 Work a few stay stitches through the pleats you have made at both sides. Fold the skirt in half lengthways with right sides together and sew a ½in (13mm) back seam up to the dots. This larger seam is to offer increased support for the tulle layers that form the train. Press the seam open and slip onto your doll or mannequin. Form the two pleats at the front carefully with your fingertips. It will take a little time to ease them into place.

2

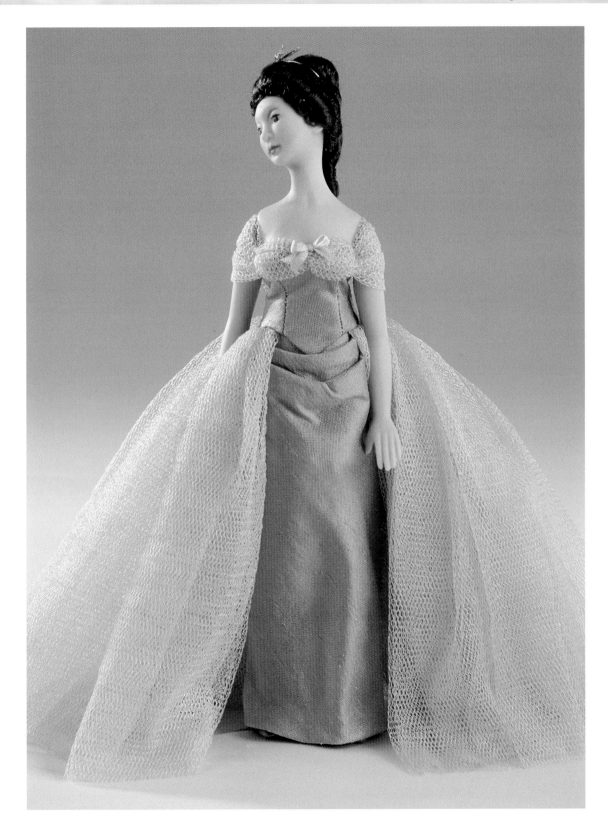

3 Turn up the bottom of the skirt so that the shoes just appear at the front. Trim the hem to ⅛in (3mm) then remove and press. Use a tiny amount of fabric glue to keep the hem in place. Slip the skirt onto the doll and oversew the remaining back edge.

4 Prepare the train by cutting a strip of tulle 40 x 3½in (1016 x 89mm). Fold under 4in (102mm) at each end of the strip and sew a gathering line along one long edge and through both layers of the folded tulle at each end. Pull the thread carefully until the top edge of this first layer measures only 1in (25mm). Pin it to the back of the skirt, ½in (13mm) at each side of the back seam so that the tulle is sitting neatly at floor level with the fold on the underside. Sew into place.

5 Cut your second tulle layer, 50 x 4½in (1270 x 114mm), and gather it in the same way, again folding under 4in (102mm) at each end and then pulling the gathering thread until the strip measures 1½in (38mm). Pin it to the back of the skirt in a half circle, making sure that the bottom edge is level with the floor all the way around, then stitch into place.

6 Cut the final layer, 60 x 5½in (1524 x 140mm), and fold the strip in half. Taper the lower edge of the strip with a gentle curve from 5½in (140mm) at the fold, which is the back of the skirt, to 5in (127mm) at the two sides. Cut straight for 8in (203mm) at the front edges as this will be folded over to gather and therefore needs to be level. (See the diagram on page 170.) Repeat the gathering stage, pulling the gathering thread until the strip measures 2in (51mm) for this layer. Pin to the back and sides of the skirt just below the waist then stitch into place.

7 Make up Bodice A with a 'v' lower front, dipped lower back and a straight neckline (see pages 66–68). Fit the bodice onto the doll.

8 Fold the tulle collar in half, bringing the two shorter sides together, and mark the centre with a pin. Fold under ⅛in (3mm) on the upper and lower edges at this centre point and gather down the centre line. Pull the thread quite tight and fasten off. Gather two more rows of stitches ½in (13mm) from the centre on each side. Pull the thread not quite so tightly and fasten off.

9 Glue the centre front and the outer gathers to the bodice of the doll. Allow each side to cover the upper arm at the front and drape downwards at the back, pinning the remainder to the centre back of the bodice. Turn the tulle under, trimming off any excess and work a few stitches to keep it in place.

10 Glue a small silk ribbon rose to the centre back and front and an extended rose to the back waist. Spray the tulle train with a light dusting of gold glitter mist hairspray.

9

10

Venetian Rhapsody

♥ ♥ ♥ Experienced

MATERIALS

♥ *14in (356mm) of 69in (1750mm) cappuccino silk tulle for the underskirt*

♥ *Rich cream silk for the gown and ivory Habutai for the skirt lining*

♥ *Narrow coffee-and-cream-coloured lace*

♥ *12 each of small coffee, cream, beige and peach roses and two extended roses in any of the four colours (see pages 70–71)*

♥ *Patterns on pages 171–173*

A touch of Italy influenced this gown. It is made from a rich cream silk and has a cappuccino tulle underskirt and coffee and cream lace trim. An abundance of silk roses in coffee, cream, beige and peach and a coffee lace tiara completes the look.

1 Make up Bodice A with a dipped lower front and back and straight neckline (see pages 66–68). Add a gathered lace edging along the entire upper and lower edges.

2 Make up the tulle underskirt following steps 1–3 of 'Rose Garden' (page 82).

3 A lining is required for the gown's skirt, as the paler shade is over a darker colour. Cut out and apply Fray Check fabric sealant to the skirt and lining. Turn under, press and glue a ⅛in (3mm) hem then a ½in (13mm) turning on both sides of the open front of the skirt and a ½in (13mm) turning on both sides of the open front of the lining.

4 Edge the two open front sides and the entire hem with lace so that just the edge is on show.

5 Place the lining and skirt together so that the lining is just behind the open front edges and secure it down these edges with a few spots of glue.

6 Gather the waist, sewing through both layers and fit onto the doll with the open front sides of the skirt edge to edge.

7 With the bodice out on a flat surface, arrange the roses along the front of the neckline. Glue one or two at the centre front, leave the rest in the order that they are to appear on the bodice. Fit the bodice before adding the remainder of the roses to the neckline.

8 Glue an extended rose to the front side waist and the back of the waist. Arrange the remaining small roses down the skirt back and one or both front edges.

Royal Ascot

♥ ♥ ♥ Experienced

MATERIALS

♥ *White silk for the gown*

♥ *1³/₄in (44mm) black lace for around the bottom of the gown with the excess tulle trimmed away to form a shaped upper edge so that the centre front has the highest peak. (Remember to Fray Check all the cut edges.)*

♥ *1in (25mm) lace in the same design and trimmed for the train*

♥ *Narrow black lace trim in the same design and trimmed for the bodice*

♥ *⁵/₈in (15mm) black and white striped ribbon for the bow and tails*

♥ *Extended roses (see pages 70–71) in black or white for the front and back waist trim*

♥ *Patterns on pages 174–175*

This is a striking creation in white silk with a shaped black lace overlay, ¹/₂in (13mm) train and striped ribbon trim. The wig is of the purest white with small black silk roses down the side of the upswept style. Her shoes are painted white with tiny black bows. A pill box hat, dolly purse and a parasol with striped ribbon trims and black roses provide the perfect accessories for a 'Royal Ascot' inspired theme (see Designer Collections, page 151).

1 Make up Bodice A with a dipped lower back and straight neckline (see pages 66–68) and edge with the trimmed narrow lace.

2 Make up a tulle petticoat following steps 1–2 of 'Rose Garden' on page 82.

3 Join the two sides of the skirt to the front, open the seams and press. With the skirt open on a flat surface, pin the lace to the lower edge with the higher peak at the centre front. Stitch or glue into place and close the back seam.

4 Gather the upper edge of the skirt and fit onto the doll pulling the gathers towards the back of the doll to form cascading folds.

5 Cut out the train, Fray Check the edges and turn under and glue a ⅛in (3mm) hem around the two sides and the lower edge. Attach the lace.

6 Gather the upper edge of the train and position at the back of the doll.

7 Fit the bodice onto the doll and trim at the back with a striped ribbon bow and silk roses. Attach an extended rose to the front side waist.

Blue Moon

♥ ♥ ♥ Experienced

MATERIALS

♥ *Sky-blue silk for the gown and ruffle base train*

♥ *20in (508mm) x 3in (76mm) strip of pale blue polyester tulle for the petticoat*

♥ *17³⁄₄in (450mm) ivory silk tulle for dyeing*

♥ *Pale blue ultra-fine glitter dust*

♥ *1 tin of Dylon cold water dye in Bahamas Blue with salt and dye fix*

♥ *Patterns on page 176*

This is a beautiful blue bridal ensemble with a gown in sky blue silk. In her hair I placed some ¹⁄₁₆in (2mm) silk ribbon roses and a curled feather. I painted blue shoes onto her feet with two tiny bow trims using the same ribbon as for the roses in her hair.

1 Make up the dye bath according to the instructions but use only half of all the stated quantities. Silk tulle and lace does not require a lot of dye as it is so fine and it will take less than the stated hour for soaking. Whilst the tulle is in the bath, carefully remove it regularly to check the colour. Once you have achieved the desired shade, pour out the dye and rinse the fabric gently in tepid water. Do not squeeze the tulle as this will cause permanent creasing; instead, lay it on a towel to remove surplus water before transferring the tulle and towel to a drying rail.

Note

Whilst dying the silk tulle, include some narrow ivory cotton lace for the corset lower trim and a piece of lace suitable for the centre of the corset front. You can also add some dyed blue lace to the upper and lower edges of the gown bodice if you wish.

2 Cut out the four skirt pattern pieces on page 176 and the flounced train in silk, apply Fray Check fabric sealant to all the edges. Leave to dry.

3 Cut a 69 x 3½in (1750 x 89mm) strip for the underskirt from the edge of the silk tulle.

4 Cut the remaining blue silk tulle into strips for the back of the dress using the layout (**A**) on the facing page and starting from the bottom first ruffle and working upwards. You may find it helpful to cut out the strips and the veil in paper first then lay the pattern pieces on the tulle according to the layout to ensure you have cut the pieces correctly. Cut the 'No Sew' veil (see page 127) from the remaining corner last of all.

5 Sew a tiny ¹⁄₁₆in (1.5mm) running stitch along one long edge of each tulle strip ⅛in (3mm) down from the top. When gathering silk tulle always go down and come up a hole in the mesh and not through the actual yarn itself as this can damage the fine tulle.

6 Mark the side edges of the tulle ruffle lines on the flounced train with a little tailor's chalk or a pin. Measure the distance from the bottom centre of the train to the placement where the centre of each ruffle is to be positioned and insert a pin at this point (marked with a star on the pattern piece). Gently pull the gathering threads in the tulle and pin the strips evenly along the appropriate tulle pinning line. Start with the bottom ruffle, pinning and sewing it into place with a small running stitch before starting with the next ruffle. Keep your stitches very small so that they are as close to invisible as possible.

7 Prepare the silk overskirt. Pin the two skirt facings to the skirt sides matching the stars on the pattern at the waist. Sew both facings into place with a ⅛in (3mm) seam using a tiny running stitch. Clip the curves up to the stitching, taking care not to cut the tiny stitches. Turn the facing through to the inside and press. Continue to press a ⅛in (3mm) hem between each facing on the lower edge of the skirt and use the tiniest amount of fabric glue to secure the hem in place.

8 Prepare to assemble the bride. Gather the length of polyester tulle and pin evenly around the doll so that the bottom of the tulle is resting on the floor. Stitch in place on the soft body of the doll. Gather the length of silk tulle and attach to the doll in the same way so that the layer is also resting upon the floor and the upper edge is just above the upper edge of the first layer. This forms the underskirt.

9 Sew a tiny gathering row of stitches along the upper edge of the ruffle gown back, pull gently to a width of 1in (25mm) then pin and stitch into place at the back of the doll's waistline so that the top of the train is just above the waistline itself.

10 Sew a tiny gathering row of stitches around the upper edge of the overskirt. Pull gently and fit around the doll so that it just meets at the back. Sew into place.

11 Make up Bodice B with a dipped lower back and front and a straight neckline (see pages 66–68). Fit the bodice onto the doll and glue the folded back edge over the other side, leaving the lower part of the bodice back open for a better fit if necessary. Add a few optional silk ribbon roses to the waist back.

12 Position the bodice on the doll and pin at the back so that the bodice fits snugly. Turn under the left side edge of the bodice back, which will overlap the right side. Remove the bodice and glue this edge. Apply some optional blue lace trim to the upper and lower edges of the bodice. Paint a thin line of glue to the upper and lower edges of the bodice and scatter with the glitter dust.

Veil	Tulle layout	6th ruffle	34 x 1in (864 x 25mm)
		5th ruffle	34 x 1in (864 x 25mm)
Fingertip length: no sew veil		4th ruffle	34 x 2in (864 x 51mm)
	7th and 8th ruffle	3rd ruffle	34 x 2in (864 x 51mm)
	23 x 1in (584 x 25mm)		
		2nd ruffle	69 x 2in (1,753 x 51mm)
		1st ruffle	69 x 2in (1,753 x 51mm)
		Petticoat ruffle	69 x 3in (1,753 x 76mm)

Hollywood Panache

MATERIALS

- ♥ *14in (356mm) of 69in (1750mm) red silk tulle and a piece for veiling if required*
- ♥ *Rich red silk for the gown*
- ♥ *Optional ruby and gold micro-dot crystals with pointed backs, or glitter dust*
- ♥ *Narrow gold lace*
- ♥ *Patterns on pages 177–178*

This is a rather romantic and dramatic red silk full-skirted gown with an integral train and raised lower front hemline, which you can extend to the full length if you wish. The tiara has baby gold teardrops and ruby crystals in a neat row, giving a half-crown effect. You could complement the gown with a dramatic red rose bouquet and veil.

1 Make up the tulle underskirt following steps 1–3 of 'Rose Garden' on page 82).

2 Join the back seam of the main skirt up to 1in (25mm) from the top. Join the skirt front onto the two sides of the skirt and press all the seams. With right sides together, join on the back. Open out the seams and press. Turn under and glue a hem, snipping a tiny cut at the two curves of the shaped front marked with a star on the pattern. Fit the skirt onto the doll.

3 Make up Bodice A with dipped lower front and 'v' shaped back (see pages 66–68). Apply a fine line of glue to the bodice, following the design on the pattern piece or your own design, then add the optional crystals or glitter dust. Fit the bodice onto the doll.

4 With right sides together, sew the two sides of the shawl collar. Press the seams and turn under a ⅛in (3mm) hem around the lower and upper edges. Fit over the bodice and secure with a little glue.

5 Complete the gown with a fabric rose and a few ribbon roses.

A Taste of Honey

MATERIALS

♥ *Honey silk taffeta*

♥ *5 extended honey silk roses*
   (see pages 70–71)

♥ *Honey and gold*
   Accent beads

♥ *118in x 3¹⁄₂in (3m x 89mm)*
   strip of soft-quality honey
   polyester tulle for underskirt

♥ *Narrow champagne lace for*
   the petticoat

♥ *Patterns on pages 179–180*

Delicate shades of honey taffeta silk and tulle, champagne lace, a hint of gold and a sprinkling of tiny champagne, gold and honey beads underpin this design. The headdress has been created with an extended silk rose, to match those in the gown, and some striped cockerel feathers, trimmed to the shape of an 'arrowhead', together with a curled feather. The honey-coloured shoes have tiny matching bows.

1

1 Make up and fit the tulle underskirt following
Step 1 of Crystal Snowflake on page 84,
adding the honey lace to the lower edge so
that it just touches the floor.

2 Make up the five-part skirt leaving the upper 1in (25mm) of the back seam open, press the seams, turn under a hem and gather the waist ⅛in (3mm) down from the upper edge.

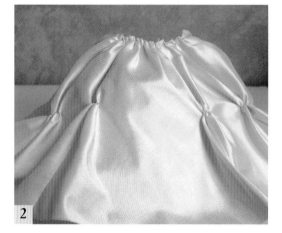

3 Mark with a pin the measurement from the lower hem on each of the five seams as indicated on the pattern pieces. Gather ⅝in (15mm) horizontally on each side of the pin. Pull the stitches to form a ruche and fasten off. Add an extended rose to each gather.

4 Fit the skirt onto the doll, easing and stitching the waist into place before closing the back and fastening off.

5 Make up Bodice A with a 'v' lower front, dipped back and straight neckline (see pages 66–68) and add a few optional beads around the neckline. Fit the bodice and place a silk bow at the back waist of the gown.

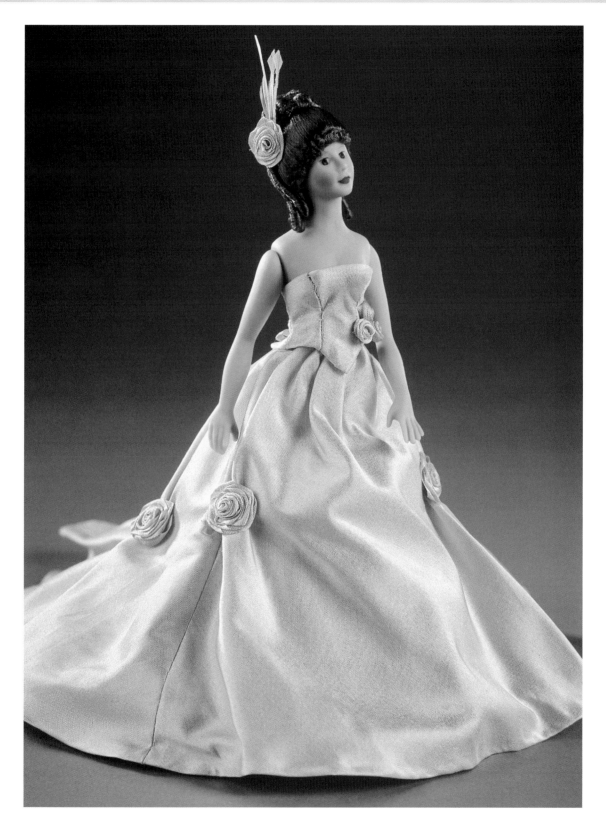

Chantilly Mist

♥ ♥ ♥ ♥ Advanced

MATERIALS

♥ *8in (203mm) of 69in (1750mm)*
ivory silk tulle for the petticoat

♥ *20in x 15in (508 x 380mm)*
ivory silk tulle for the
gathered bustle

♥ *Ivory silk for the gown*

♥ *Piece of Chantilly lace with*
a fringed border for the skirt
overlay and a small piece
for the bolero jacket

♥ *Patterns on pages 181–183*

The palest ivory silk and soft Chantilly lace form this
pretty creation with an integral cathedral-length train.
The back of the gown has a silk tulle gathered bustle.
A delicate lace bolero jacket completes the ensemble.
This dress is perfect if you would like to try either a
cathedral- or monarch-length veil.

1 Make up Bodice A with a dipped lower back and straight
neckline (see pages 66–68).

2 Prepare the doll's petticoat with a 3½in (89mm) strip of
silk tulle and a 4½in (114mm) upper layer. Fit as for
the first two steps of 'Rose Garden' on page 82.

3 Pin and sew the skirt pieces and close the back
seam leaving a gap for fitting onto the doll. Turn
under and glue a ⅛in (3mm) hem and add a row of
gathering stitches around the waist. Fit onto the doll
and close the remainder of the back seam.

4 Place the pattern for the skirt overlay onto
the lace so that the fringed edge is at the
bottom between the points indicated on the
pattern. Cut the remainder of the lace and
apply a little Fray Check fabric sealant to
the cut edges.

5 Apply a thread edge to the two outer curved sides of the overlay between the two stars marked on the pattern on each side and trim the outer tips of the fringe towards the beginning of the thread outline, also shown on the pattern.

6 Gather the upper edge of the overlay between the two stars on the top edge. Fit the overlay onto the doll.

8

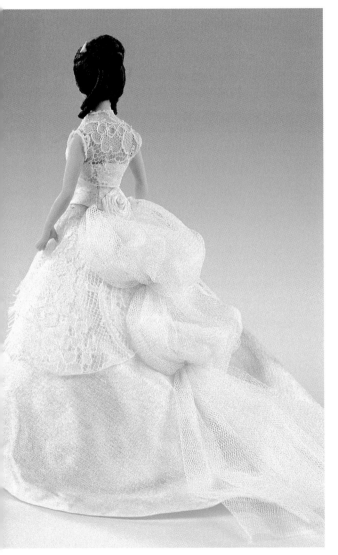

7 Gather the upper edge of the 20in (508mm) long bustle. Sew another gathering row 3in (76mm) down and a third 3in (75mm) down from that. Pull the upper thread until the width is 1in (25mm) and stitch to the centre back of the skirt.

8 Pull the gathers in the next row down and pin so the bustle is formed with a gentle dip. Repeat for the final gathers. Glue the gathers into place on the back seam and fit the bodice.

9 Cut out the bolero in lace and glue the side seams together. When thoroughly dry turn through to the right side and apply a thread outline to the arm holes and the entire lower edge.

10 Slip the bolero onto the doll and, if necessary, keep in place at the side of the bodice front with a tiny dot of glue. Add extended roses or bows (see pages 70–73) to the front side waist, the bodice back and the bustle gathers.

Ocean Dreams

❤ ❤ ❤ ❤ Advanced

MATERIALS

❤ *6in (152mm) of 69in (1750mm) aqua silk tulle*

❤ *Ice blue silk for the petticoat and gown*

❤ *Small selection of tiny seashells and aqua crystals or glitter dust*

❤ *Pearly aqua Accent beads*

❤ *Small quantity of narrow silvery lace*

❤ *Patterns on page 183*

This is a mystical mermaid-style gown, which is influenced by the depths of the sea. It is made in ice blue silk with silver lace and has tiny shells and an aqua tulle fishtail skirt. She wears a lace tiara with a shell trim.

1 Make up Petticoat 1 (see page 63) with ½in (13mm) longer darts for a tight fit and leaving the top 1in (25mm) of the back seam open. Trim the darts and apply Fray Check fabric sealant. Slip onto the doll and close.

2 Cut two strips of tulle that are the full width of the fabric, 3in (76mm) wide and 2½in (63mm) wide. Gather both strips and attach to the lower edge of the petticoat, the shorter strip first, so that it touches the floor, then at the back pull gently down to form a fishtail.

4 Make up the skirt in the same way as the petticoat, press the seams open and turn under a hem. Attach some silvery lace to the lower edge just peeping out at the bottom.

3 Repeat for the upper layer so that it also touches the floor at the front but points downwards at the back.

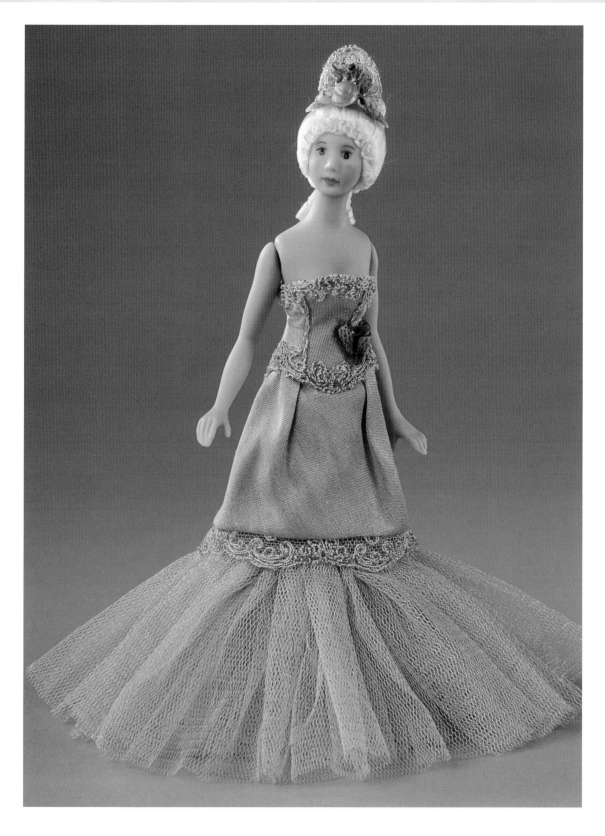

5 Make up Bodice A with a lower dipped front, 'v' lower back and straight neckline (see pages 66–68). Trim the lower edge with silvery lace, which has been trimmed and shaped by cutting away the excess tulle.

6 Fit the skirt and bodice, leaving the lower part of the bodice open at the back, and add a few acqua crystals or glitter dust and optional Accent beads around the necklline.

7 Cut out the lower back drape and Fray Check the edges. Add some trimmed silver lace to the top of the outer edges and gather the upper edge. Pull the gathers tightly and attach to the centre back of the skirt with some sea shells on top of the gathers. I placed a group of shells at the side waist.

Pumpkins and Butterflies

♥ ♥ ♥ ♥ Advanced

MATERIALS

- ♥ *14in (356mm) of 69in (1750mm) ivory silk tulle for the skirt*
- ♥ *7in (178mm) of pale pink 5½in (140mm) decorative polyester tulle for panniers*
- ♥ *4 x ½in (102 x 13mm) silk Dupion without interfacing for the shawl collar*
- ♥ *⅜in (10mm) pale pink organza ribbon*
- ♥ *Small piece of organza fabric and a tiny piece of bondaweb for the butterfly*
- ♥ *¼in (7mm), ³⁄₁₆in (4mm) and ¹⁄₁₆in (2mm) silk ribbon in baby pink*
- ♥ *6–7 tiny gold butterfly nail charms*
- ♥ *Gold glitter mist hair spray*
- ♥ *Pattern on page 183*

The titled bridal salon design brings together a romantic Cinderella-inspired gown with an ivory silk tulle skirt and pale pink fine polyester tulle faux panniers. The panniers are tied at the back with a bouquet of silk and organza ribbon roses, tiny gold butterflies and an organza butterfly. The pretty fitted bodice has a shawl collar trimmed with tiny bows and butterflies. Her gold tiara has pearly pink baby teardrop leaves, gold ivy and a central butterfly. Her 'glass' slippers were painted with ivory acrylic then an adhesive was applied in stages before dusting with pink ultra-fine glitter dust. Tiny ivory silk ribbon bows provide the finishing touch.

1 Make up the tulle skirt following Steps 1–3 of 'Rose Garden' on page 82. Follow the preparation tip overleaf then pin the side panniers to the waist of the doll towards the back and level with the top of the last tier of tulle. Stitch into place. (See page 74 for an illustration showing the position of the panniers.)

2 Make up Bodice A with dipped lower back, 'v' shaped lower front and straight neckline (see pages 66–68). Fit the bodice.

Preparation Tip

Unlike silk tulle, polyester tulle is stiff and will not drape. However, for this gown you need a fabric for the side panniers with a little body. To prepare the panniers:

1 Cut the polyester tulle in half lengthways.

2 Round off the lower corners of each piece and gather the 2½in (63mm) upper edges. Pull the gathers tightly and then fasten off the threads.

3 Pull the lengths of tulle tightly and sandwich between the pages of a heavy book.

Add more weight on top of the book and leave overnight. This will flatten the tulle and whilst adding body with the tulle itself, the drapes will be much easier to sculpt into shape. Use this method for other similar projects when you need to drape a tulle with a little more stiffness than silk tulle but without the over stiffness of regular polyester tulle. The decorative-quality tulle is softer and therefore more suitable than other dress tulle for miniature costuming.

3 Close the back seam in the shawl collar, turn to the right side and press the seam open. Turn under and press ⅛in (3mm) hem on the top and bottom edges. Holding the seam, fold the collar in half to find the centre front and mark the centre with a pin. Place the shawl on the doll with the centre front and back seam in place. Mark both sides of the arm with a pin. Remove the collar and gather vertically where the centre front is and each side of the arms. Glue the collar into position. Add a ¹⁄₁₆in (2mm) silk ribbon bow to the centre front, centre back and each shoulder of the collar. I added a gold butterfly to the centre back.

4 Place one of the tulle panniers over the other and gather them together as one, 3½in (89mm) from the lower edge. They are gathered in this way because a flatter gather is needed for this. Pull the gathered thread quite tightly and fasten off.

5 Sandwich two pieces of organza with some bondaweb large enough for the butterfly and cut it out using the pattern piece. Add gold acrylic paint highlights to the outer edge of the wing. Fold the butterfly in half and attach to the back of the waist with a pink ¼in (7mm) silk ribbon bow in the centre and a gold butterfly charm on the top.

6 Add a large organza rose to the gathers in the panniers. Place a ¼in (7mm) silk ribbon bow underneath. Add some gold butterflies to the rose. (See picture on page 74). At the front of the dress place an extended ³⁄₁₆in (4mm) silk ribbon rose to the side of the waist with another gold butterfly on top and one on the opposite side of the waist.

7 Complete the dress with a spray of glitter mist hairspray.

Accessories

Weddings today are such a huge business, and I'm often amazed at the enormous and increasing range of wedding paraphernalia that is available.

Of course, the best news for us is that almost everything that is available for real weddings can be reproduced in miniature. The list is quite extensive and there's no reason to miss out on anything.

In this section you'll find a wonderful array of accessories to get you started, including jewellery, lingerie, fans, and floral arrangements, plus other accessories to complement the gowns featured in this book.

Tools and Materials

The tools and materials that you will require
to complete the accessories in this section are
as follows:

- ♥ a base wire for the tiaras in silver
  and gold – $^1/_{32}$in (0.6mm) or gauge 22 craft wire
  is ideal for this purpose
- ♥ 28 gauge wire in several colours to thread
  tiny beads
- ♥ various shades of ultra-fine glitter dust
- ♥ no-hole beads and pearls
- ♥ tiny pin-head flat-backed crystals, micro crystals
  and pearls
- ♥ petite embroidery beads
- ♥ tiny etched brass leaves
- ♥ metallic and pearl punched paper leaves; maple
  leaf, ivy leaf and baby teardrop are my favourites

- ♥ silk ribbon, roses and rose maker
- ♥ pestle and morter for grinding pot pourri
- ♥ micro cake decorating stamens
- ♥ assorted feathers
- ♥ metallic thread
- ♥ pearl polymer clay and wooden toothpicks,
  decorative cocktail sticks or metal rod for
  the Venetian mask handles
- ♥ bent-nose tweezers are essential
- ♥ cocktail sticks and toothpicks for applying
  tiny amounts of glue and spacing miniature parts
- ♥ mouse mat and small embossing stylus for
  shaping the miniature paper leaves
- ♥ thick PVA glue to apply paper, small crystals,
  glitter dust and beads
- ♥ a needle file to shape the Venetian mask
  polymer clay shapes during construction.

You will also need a good-quality bonding adhesive to firmly attach metal leaves and the crystal metal backs to the tiara wire and the mask sticks to the painted polymer clay masks. I use 'Zap A Gap'. I have found it to be the best as long as you follow the precautions outlined on the bottle. Always put a little of the glue in a dish and apply with the tip of a cocktail stick. Lastly, a block of oasis glued onto a piece of card is perfect for keeping tiny accessories in place whilst working on them and waiting for parts to dry.

There is one new addition to my work basket which I can thoroughly recommend: Swarovski crystal dust and chippings called Swarovski Accents. I have been a fan of Swarovski crystal for quite some time and have especially loved working with the beads. However, whilst I could easily find some miniature ornaments and the chandeliers made from this beautiful crystal for the salon, I couldn't find any suitable crystals for miniature dressmaking. You can imagine how delighted I was to discover this product. They are available in clear, red, deep blue and a mix of colours. When the light catches them they are simply stunning. Within the phial there are crystals of various sizes, from ⅛in (3mm) down to the tiniest of pieces no bigger than some craft glitter. The graduating sizes make it perfect for miniature jewellery displays, necklaces, tiaras, Venetian masks and, of course, miniature wedding gowns, where you can glue them individually into place where beads would normally be sewn.

Paint Finishes

The Venetian masks, some of the shoes, parasols and a few other salon items have been finished with metallic acrylic paint. There are several shades on the market and this is just a short guide of the product colours I have used. The metallic acrylic paints are by Winsor and Newton, Galleria Series 2 and Finity Series 3 and an acrylic gesso primer. Both series are semi-transparent and will need two to three coats.

Series 2 Silver is my usual choice for silver miniatures with a pretty silvery sheen which is not too dark.

Series 2 Gold has a deep rich coppery or orange hue.

Series 2 Old Gold is the shade of gold I usually use with a deep brown hue. It is the nearest in shade to the liquid gold leaf if you need a match.

Series 3 Silver is slightly paler than the Series 2 silver with a lovely pearl finish.

Series 3 Dark Silver is, as the name suggests, a dark grey pewter colour and not one I would use for 'silver' miniatures but perfect when simulating pewter.

Series 3 Gold is a bright yellow opulent gold, the shade you would use for miniature gilding. It is the closest shade to real gold leaf.

Series 3 Antique Gold has an unusual yellow-green hue and is quite stunning.

Series 3 Renaissance Gold is quite coppery and a slightly paler shade of Series 2 gold.

Veils and Veiling

A bridal veil is, without doubt, the most elegant and beautiful bridal accessory. The history of the bridal veil can be traced right back to Roman times when they tended to be red in colour and used solely for the purpose of shielding the bride from the gaze of evil spirits who may have tried to do her harm. Today the veil is simply considered to be the perfect complement to the bride's gown.

Veiling Fabric

There are five main fabrics that are suitable for veiling, but I would recommend only one for miniatures. Full-size veils tend to be made from stiff fabrics such as polyester tulle. This tulle will stick out horizontally if used on miniature brides. Point d'esprit is a softer, more fluid cotton net with an all-over spotted design. I have used it in the past, but the spots are not quite to scale in size or spacing, which is something to consider. The very soft fabrics include silk tulle or a lace such as Chantilly. The silk tulle with a slight stretch is the finest, though, and will enable you to achieve the best results.

Lengths of Veil

There are seven lengths of bridal veil. The blusher or face veil generally covers only the face. Worn on its own or as a top tier for a longer-length veil, it is the part normally lifted back at the end of the ceremony. The next length reaches the shoulder. With arms by your sides, the elbow length is next followed by the fingertip length. The ballet length reaches mid-calf and the chapel length rests upon the floor. The longest veil is the cathedral length and this is for the most formal of weddings. This particular style, which trails the floor, can extend considerably in length when it becomes the Royal Cathedral or Monarch. One only has to observe a Royal wedding to see the difference in the length of this veil.

Tiers and Styles

As well as varying in length, the veil can be made with either a single tier, which is the basic drape, or have multiple tiers. Generally, a multi-tiered veil is formed with a shorter upper tier graduating to longer lengths for each tier underneath. For example, a shoulder-length tier could have an elbow-length tier beneath it with either a fingertip or ballet-length tier as a bottom layer. Alternatively, a fingertip tier can have a chapel- and cathedral-length tier below it. One tip to remember when making a multi-tiered veil, or indeed anything with layers of fabric, is to gather each tier separately then place each one on top of the other before sewing them firmly together with tiny running stitches. If you place the fabric layers on top of one another first then gather them together as one the fabric will not sit right or fall in soft drapes. Also, remember that the more tiers you add in miniature, the less 'airy' the veil will appear.

I think two tiers at most are the best for miniature brides. You may need to experiment to see which you prefer, though.

The Basic Drape

On the facing page there is a guide to the length and width of tulle rectangle you will need to cut to make a single-layer veil. If you wish the veil to fall from the top of the head, cut the longer length of each style. The shorter length is to be used for veils which are to fall from the base of the head, perhaps under a raised hairstyle.

For each of the basic drapes listed below, fold the tulle in half lengthways and round off the outer corner before gathering ⅛in (3mm) from the upper edge.

Blusher:

A tulle circle 3⅛in (80mm) in diameter for a single veil to be worn on its own or a 4in wide x 1½in long (approximately 100 x 40mm) rectangle with rounded-off corners on the lower edge for an upper tier on a layered veil.

Shoulder:

120mm wide x 50–60mm long (4¾ x 2–2⅜in)

Elbow:

150mm wide x 80–100mm long (6 x 3⅛–4in)

Fingertip:

200mm wide x 100–120mm long (7¾ x 3⅛–4¾in)

Ballet:

250mm wide x 120–140mm long (7¾ x 4¾–5½in)

Chapel:

250mm wide x 160–180mm long (7¾ x 6⁵⁄₁₆in)

Cathedral:

250mm wide x 250–400mm long (7¾ x 7¾–15¾in) (see right)

No Sew

This veil is ideal for miniatures. Cut an elongated oval from silk tulle, using the pattern on page 184; I've included three lengths. Pinch the spot marked with a star on the pattern and attach it to the bottom of a raised hairstyle. You can also use this method to create a circular veil, using the mantilla measurements on the following page but pinching almost half way down so the top half of the circle is just above the lower edge of the bottom of the circle.

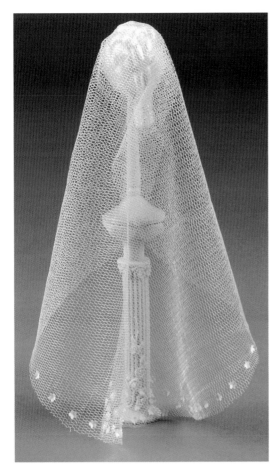

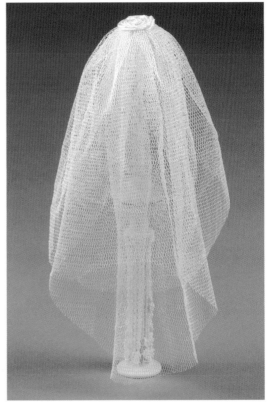

Mantilla

Another style of veil that consists of a single tier is the mantilla (pronounced man-tey-a) which is circular in shape and often made from lace in real life for a softer drape. The bride attaches the edge of the mantilla just above her forehead, allowing the remainder of the veil to form a circular frame at the back. As with the basic single drape veil, the mantilla can also vary in length from fingertip to cathedral length. A circle with a 4¾in (120mm) diameter will make up into a fingertip-length mantilla, a 5½in (140mm) circle will make a ballet-length mantilla and a 6⁵⁄₁₆in (180mm) circle will give a chapel-length mantilla. A longer-length mantilla in miniature form may result in a veil which has too much fabric in its appearance rather than having a light and airy quality, although it is, of course, a matter of personal taste. You can always try the longer mantilla then trim it down to a narrower style. You can also edge your veil with some single cupped babies' breath petals.

Cascade

The cascade is a style of veil that is in between the basic drape and mantilla. It has much shorter sides than the basic drape but is a little wider and more circular in shape. To achieve an effective cascade-style veil, try a fingertip, ballet or chapel length. This is a lovely style for displaying on a veil stand in a miniature bridal shop. Use the pattern grid on page 185 to cut double-tier cascade-style veils.

Pouf

The pouf or frou frou is a style which can be worn on its own as a headdress in the form of a small ruffled lace or tulle frill or it can be added to the top of the basic drape. It usually sits at the back of the head. To add it to the top of any basic drape veil, add a further ¾in (about 20mm) to the upper edge. Fold over ½in (about 12mm) and sew the gathering line ⅛in (3mm) up from the raw edge and ⅜in (10mm) down from the fold.

Dragonfly

The dragonfly or angel is a design with a central drop and shorter sides, just like the centre of a dragonfly with its upswept lower wings or the shape of a stereotypical angel with arms outstretched upwards. The tulle veil has a pleated and tapered centre then it is gathered at the top, as for the basic drape. The pattern provided on page 185 is for three lengths: a fingertip, ballet and chapel. If allowed to sweep the floor then you lose the effect of the centre fold drop. Using the diagram provided, first fold the veil down the centre lengthways and open it out, marking the top

and bottom of the centre with a pin. On one side measure 1in (25mm) from the centre and mark with a pin. Take this pin to the centre and make sure this fold is equal all the way down to the bottom of the veil. Measure 1¹⁄₁₆in (27mm) from the edge of the first centre fold and mark with a pin. Take this pin to ¹⁄₁₆in (1.5mm) behind the first fold then allow the rest of the veil side or to lie flat out at the side. Pin the tails into place then repeat for the opposite side. Starting at the outer tip of the right wing, sew a row of gathering stitches right across the upper edge through all the pleats ⅛in (3mm) down from the top. Fasten off the thread and place the folded veil between some fine cotton lawn and place inside a heavy book. Arrange the veil into its pleated folds all the way down and leave overnight to hold the pleats. You can spray the completed veil with a little glitter hair mist.

Headdresses

Once the veils have been created you must turn your attention to the 'crowning' feature. These miniature tiaras take some patience; they are definitely not to be rushed. Each leaf, petal and tiny crystal needs to be applied singly and allowed to dry. I have used quite a range of materials and I'm sure you'll find lots more; this is just a starting point for you.

Tiaras

The Tiara Base:

1 To shape the tiara base wire you will need a tubular object with a diameter of about ½in (13mm). I use a simple lip-gloss case for this purpose but you could use a piece of dowel. Bend the ¹⁄₃₂in (0.6mm) wire around it and remove.

2 You may find it easier to work on the tiara with a short piece of excess wire to hold, so just cut the wire at this stage until you have had time to experiment. Alternatively, cut the two side edges of the wire to form a shape that is slightly larger than a half circle. The base can be further trimmed back once complete to fit a particular doll or hairstyle.

3 When you have formed the base for the tiara, you can begin applying the decorations.

There are four basic styles that form the basis of the miniature tiara:

Style 1

These tiaras are for the beginner and, although extremely easy, are both grand and effective. They are created with just a tiny scrap of lace.

1 Simply cut the edge off a lace scallop or make up your own shape from this part of a lace and apply Fray Check fabric sealant to all the edges before gluing it to the tiara base.

2 You can either use metallic lace, or paint and highlight some plain lace for this style; both are equally effective.

3 You can add an optional silk ribbon or parchment rose to the centre.

Style 2

These tiaras are formed with a base centre either from brass leaves or paper leaf and flower shapes and a crystal, pearl and /or a sprinkle of glitter dust. I made the tiara for 'La Dolce Vita' in this way (see above).

1 First cut a stem of three leaves from the end of a fern sheet and glue this to the centre of a tiara base with the bonding adhesive.

2 Add a single leaf at each side on the base of the tiara itself, gluing only the stem of the leaf and not the whole leaf, as you will next glue two leaves just beneath them.

3 Glue a final leaf to the front at an angle and use a toothpick to keep it upright, taking great care not to get any of the glue on the toothpick.

4 As I made this tiara for a gold-themed bride, I added just a little glitter dust to the centre of the leaves as a highlight.

Alternatives

♥ Make a variation on this design by adding a central pearl instead of the eighth leaf (see above). Simply glue five flat-backed pink pin-head crystals around the pearl at the base of each leaf and add a rose-pink glitter dust highlight to each leaf.

♥ Cut the pointed tips from three long teardrops and glue them behind a maple leaf (see top). Apply two shades of blue Swarovski crystals to the base in the following order: one medium aqua crystal in the centre with a small cobalt crystal at each side and one above it, then a tiny cobalt crystal on each side of the small cobalt crystals.

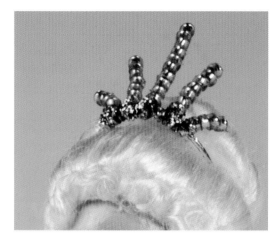

Style 3

These tiaras are formed with either looped or single-strand wires and beads. A little trickier then the brass- or paper-leaf base, they are made by threading and gluing some petite glass beads or pearls in decreasing numbers. They can have five to nine beading wires but it's perhaps best to begin with five. The wires can all be straight, like a regal crown, or you can bend them outwards from a straight central wire to create a sunburst effect.

1 First make up your base and cut five 2in (51mm) lengths of beading wire which will be trimmed later.

2 Carefully hold the edge of your first wire behind the base pointing downwards. Bring the wire up at the front and bend it around the base three times, finishing with an upward point at the front. Do not cut the wire yet but add a little bonding glue to hold the twists in place. Repeat this stage with all five wires, allowing each to dry before proceeding with the next.

3 Thread some beads onto the middle wire to a height of approximately ³⁄₈in (10mm), gluing the last bead into position before cutting the wire just a whisker longer and bending the tip of the wire backwards.

4 Thread the wires on each side of the central one with beads to a height of ⁵⁄₁₆in (8mm) and the final two wires to a height of ¹⁄₄in (6mm).

5 You can add some glitter dust to the base of the tiara over the wires but it is not essential, as even real tiaras have this on view.

Style 4

These are the most ornate of tiaras and are formed with a base of leaves or shapes, some wired beads and crystals between them, and pearls or glitter dust around the base. You will need to follow the instructions for the previous styles and always allow each stage to dry thoroughly. Plan your arrangement first so that you can prepare the components beforehand.

Crowns

A bridal crown is really just an extension of the tiara, as it completes the circle and, as such, can be decorated in the same way. To make a simple contemporary crown, you will need a plain silver or gold-coloured ring with an approximate diameter of ½in (13mm) and a collection of the embellishments used for the tiaras. You can have a simple circle of paper leaves with some crystal and glitter-dust highlights, a circle of the wired beads or a combination of the two. A full circle of the tiny brass leaves applied singly and overlapping with glitter dust and crystal highlights also looks quite elegant.

Silk and Organza Headdresses

Bows

Perhaps the simplest headdress, which is still very effective, is a beautifully formed organza bow.

1 Make the bow with a bow maker and leave diagonally cut tails.

2 For extra effect, thread a few tiny, cupped, five-petal flower shapes with a ⅛in (3mm) space between each and held in place with a dot of glue. Allow them to cascade down the back of the veil from the underside of the knot of the bow. Add to the back of the head and flatten the tails around the shape of the doll's head so that they don't stick out.

3 You can add a few ¹⁄₁₆in (1.5mm) pearls to the knot of the bow if using a plain ribbon, but I find the lovely striped Ruban Ombrelle organza ribbon, used for the headdress shown here, quite striking on its own.

Note

If using one-sided paper leaves, remember to paint the back of them with a suitable silver or gold acrylic paint as they will be on view.

Roses

Equally simple yet also effective is a band of five ¹⁄₁₆in (2mm) silk ribbon roses across the top of a veil (see directly below). Larger silk roses also make a dramatic headdress if placed on the side of the doll's head with either a curled feather or a miniature 'arrow head' feather cut from the base of a striped cockerel feather. This forms the headdress for 'A Taste of Honey' (see bottom).

Another pretty headdress can be made with one large ½in (12mm) diameter silk ribbon rose and two smaller ones all made from ³⁄₁₆in (4mm) silk ribbon and three tiny cake decorating stamens. This particular headdress looks lovely perched at the top of a bun hairstyle that has been curled at the nape of the neck, (see directly below) and can be worn either with or without a veil. Simply glue one small rose to each side of the large rose. Trim the stamens so that there are three at each side falling from the smaller roses. Similar designs with a smaller central rose are suitable for bridesmaids, and although the cake stamens are only available in white, ivory or yellow, you can paint the edges with acrylic or pearlised fabric paints.

Another use for silk roses is to apply ¹⁄₁₆in (2mm) ribbon single roses to a raised hairstyle as shown on 'Blue Moon' (see bottom). Parchment roses are perfect when placed at either size of the head for older styles of veils.

Floral Rings and 'V' Bands

Floral rings, suitable for brides and their maids, are made with a few circles of thin cake wire which comes in two colours: white and green. I use the white for silk ribbon flowers and the green for 'real' flowers for the 'fresh flower' look. 'V' bands are a particular favourite of mine and they are usually formed simply with a curved wire.

Floral Rings

1 For the former of the two, wrap some white cake wire three times around a cylindrical shape with a diameter of ¾in (approx. 20mm). Remove the circlet and cut the wire in the same place as the start of the wire.

2 Glue some ³⁄₁₆in (4mm) ribbon over the join in the wire at a slight angle then wrap the ribbon around it, covering the entire wire until you are back at the starting point. Glue firmly in place.

3 Add tiny ¹⁄₁₆in (2mm) silk ribbon roses around the ring and some tails at the back using the same ribbon as for the roses. You can use more than one colour of rose, alternating them around the ring with some tiny velvet leaves in a pastel shade or traditional forest green.

To make a 'fresh flower' ring you will need an assortment of parchment roses, buds and leaves.

1 Start with a 3½in (approx. 90mm) length of green cake wire and form a very small ⅛in (3mm) hook at one side. Twist your first rose around the stem, cut it after twisting approximately ³⁄₁₆in (about 5mm), and glue into place.

2 Continue along the wire until the spray is long enough to fit around your doll's hairstyle. Cut the last rose at its base and glue it on top of the twists from the penultimate rose. This will ensure that the ring has roses all the way around.

3 Glue small leaf shapes between the roses to fill any gaps made by the twists.

4 Make another tiny hook and bend the spray into a round shape.

5 Slot a little ¹⁄₁₆in (2mm) silk ribbon through the hooks, tie and finish with a bow and tails.

'V' Bands

1 Make up a circle of white cake wire as for the floral ring.

2 Place the circlet on a flat surface. Form a 'V' shape by holding the circle where the two edges of the wire are and gently pull the opposite inside edge with a fingertip into a teardrop shape. Form the bottom of the teardrop into a more acute 'V' shape by nipping the point. Now straighten the part of the circle opposite the 'V' so that you have a triangle.

3 Starting at the top of the teardrop, glue the edge of some ³⁄₁₆in (4mm) silk ribbon to the wire over the cut ends and begin winding the ribbon all the way around. Cut the ribbon and secure with a tiny dot of glue.

4 On each of the three sides of the shape, slightly arch the centre so that it will sit snugly on the doll's head. Thread a tiny bead and sew it to the underside of the 'V', allowing it to fall at the tip.

5 These particular shaped headdresses look lovely with a pouf-topped veil. Attach the veil to the back of the band and add a tiny silk ribbon rose to each side. You can also thread a length of babies' breath cupped flowers on a length of thread, gluing each one with approximately ¹⁄₄in (6mm) space between them. Make up two or three strands to fall at each side.

Caps and Hats

A silk-covered cap decorated with tiny flowers and pearls or a bridal hat, which is the perfect accompaniment for a dress suit, both serve as an ideal base for a basic drape veil with a pouf top:

1 Cut the little cap from 'Permastiff' shirt canvas using the pattern piece on page 186 and make a tiny cut as indicated.

2 Cross one edge over the other with a ¹⁄₁₆in (2mm) overlap and glue these two sides together. When dry, cover the cap with silk, applying some glue to the upper surface only.

3 Turn the cap over and trim to ⅛in (3mm) all around the edge. Snip the curves and begin folding over and gluing each tab in turn to the underside of the cap. You can add a layer of very fine lace over the silk layer in the same way or, alternatively, add a tiny motif cut from a piece of lace after applying Fray Check to the edges.

4 Cut a cap lining in silk using the pattern on page 186 and snip the little cut before applying Fray Check to all edges. Snip the curves, fold in and press a ⅛in (3mm) hem all the way around and secure with tiny dots of glue.

5 Overlap and secure the little shaped back so that the hemmed side is on the 'outside' of the dome and glue to the underside of the cap. Trim the edge with lace.

6 A pouf veil is my choice for this headdress and you can also add some babies' breath trails.

I have used a silk hat from my collection for the headdress shown (below left) but you can make your own using a hat former or preformed 'Aida' shaped hat, both available from me at the address on page 188. The hat shape can be covered with pleated chiffon and dressed with ribbons, roses and tiny leaves cut from pearly paper. The veil to hang from a small hat is usually quite long, rectangular in shape, and about 5–6in (125–150mm) wide.

A pill-box hat is a lovely easy-to-make design:

1 Cut a strip of card ³⁄₁₆in wide x 2½in long (5 x 63mm) and a strip of silk ³⁄₈in wide x 2¾in long (10 x 70mm). Apply Fray Check to all the edges of the silk.

2 Place the card centrally on the silk then fold the silk over at the upper and lower edge. Glue, leaving one side edge unglued. Bring the two side edges together, overlap the join with the spare silk.

3 Add miniature roses, bows, feathers and add an optional veil cut from a rectangle as for the hat veil.

137

Venetian Masks and Jewellery

Once associated with masquerades, the theatre and Venice, masks have since risen in popularity as a bridal accessory. Combine them with sparkling jewellery for extra effect.

Masks

1 The face of the miniature mask is made from polymer clay which has been evenly rolled out to a thickness of $\frac{1}{16}$in (1.5mm).

2 Using the template provided on page 186, trace and cut out the shape of the face mask in thin card. Cover both sides of the card template in sticky tape or sticky-back plastic to protect it whilst making it easier to remove from the cut polymer clay shape.

3 Press the template gently onto the rolled-out polymer clay then use a sharp craft knife to cut around the mask and remove the eyelets. If your mask is not very neat at this stage do not worry.

4 First trim very obvious rough edges after removing the template. Slide the pointed edge of a cocktail stick centrally under the space between the eyes on the lower edge to form the shape where the nose will be whilst gently shaping the top of the mask on the top of the stick with your fingertips.

5 Now half bake the mask for approximately ten minutes at 250°F (130°C) or gas mark 1–2. Remove the mask from the oven and allow to cool. Gently file away any remaining rough edges and use a needle file to clean out the eyes. Put back in the oven for a further 5–10 minutes then allow to cool.

6 If using a cocktail stick for a handle, cut it to a length of 2in (51mm) from the shaped end and file to a point again. If using a toothpick, file it quite thinly and round off the lower, wider side of the stick. Prepare a brass rod handle by cutting it to a length of 2in (51mm). File one end round and smooth and the other flat before adding a bead to it to form the handle. In all three styles, glue the mask to the rod at an angle. Paint the wooden sticks and mask with your chosen metallic acrylic paint.

7 Now decorate the mask using the following: leaf shapes, crystals and glitter dust across the brow, $\frac{1}{16}$in (1.5mm) pearls around the eyes, curled and cut feathers applied just behind the top of the handle, crystals and glitter dust down the upper part of the handle and a tassel for the base.

Jewels and Chokers

The forms I have used to display the tiny necklaces
are made by Heidi Ott (see details on page 189).
They are perfect for a shop display and are
available in black or white. There are three basic
styles of necklace:

Style 1

These are made with a continuous line of crystals
or pearls. Graduate a row of Swarovski crystals
or set a central cabochon with a row of $\frac{1}{16}$in
(1.5mm) pearls.

Style 2

This style is made with either a half or full circlet
of wire to simulate a metallic chain. The particular
design shown here has a half circle of gold wire
with a fine line of glitter dust and three central flat-
backed pin-head crystals.

Style 3

This category includes decorative chokers. Glue
a circle of ribbon with the overlap at the
back or a hand-tatted lace choker around a doll
or necklace stand. Make a small bow and
glue it over the join in the ribbon. At the front of
the chokers add a small rose, pearl droplet or
butterfly either in the centre or to the side.

Lingerie and Lace

I've chosen to include instructions for a corset, bra, suspender and panties. These four items form a basic bridal set but you can make a myriad of pretty coordinated sets from the basic pattern. Also included is a pretty nightgown, which you can place in a little box for a counter in the salon, or pack in a suitcase for the Memories cameo on page 55.

MATERIALS

♥ *Chantilly lace or similar all-over lace for the corset panel, panties and suspender*
♥ *Silk for the corset and the bra and nightgown cups*
♥ *Small piece of iron-on Vilene for the lower cup shapes*
♥ *Suitable lace with a 1½in (38mm) scallop to form the upper cups of the lingerie*
♥ *⅛in (3mm) lace (this can be cut from the bottom of some deeper lace then apply Fray Check fabric sealant to the cut edge)*
♥ *⅝in (16mm) lace for the bra base, the corset trim and the nightgown cup sides*
♥ *¹⁄₃₂in (1mm) German lacet ribbon*
♥ *¹⁄₁₆in (2mm) silk ribbon for tiny bows and the nightgown straps*
♥ *7in wide x 4in long (178 x 102mm) piece of pretty muslin for the nightgown skirt*
♥ *Fine embroidery floss for thread outlining*
♥ *Patterns on page 186*

The Corset

1 Cut the five main pattern pieces: four back and front parts in silk, and a centre front panel in lace. Add Fray Check fabric sealant to all the edges.

2 Using just a little glue, join the two fronts with the lace panel in the centre, overlapping the edges of the front pieces with the lace panel – just under ¹⁄₁₆in (1.5mm) is best.

3 With right sides together, join the front to the backs with a ¹⁄₁₆in (1.5mm) side seam. Press the seams open.

4 At the back, turn under and glue a ¹⁄₁₆in (1.5mm) hem on the left side which will be stuck over the right side eventually.

5 To form the cups, press a little iron-on Vilene interfacing onto a small piece of silk and cut out two 'leaf'-shaped lower cup parts using the pattern on page 186

6 Apply glue to the very edge of the rounded upper front of the corset where the two lower cups will fit and attach the cups keeping the rounded shape.

7 Cut two scallops of 'upper cup lace' and trim the scalloped edge to a depth of ¼in (6mm). Attach this to the lower cups with the centre 'v' part of the scalloped edge to the centre of the two lower cups, applying glue to the upper edges of the lower cups and keeping the lace taut to form the rounded full cup shape. Trim the lace at the sides of the corset in line with the upper edge.

8 Apply Fray Check to the edge of some lacet ribbon and starting at the back, glue the ribbon around the upper edge of the corset to the start of the cups. Cut the ribbon and apply a little Fray Check then repeat at the other side.

9 Apply Fray Check to the cut edge of some more ribbon and attach to the edge of each side of the lace panel. Place the ribbon underneath the cups from one side to the other, crossing it at the centre and gluing the edges to the inside of the corset.

10 Gather the upper edge of some ⅝in (16mm) lace and glue evenly around the lower edge of the corset. Make sure you glue only the very edge of the lace to the edge of the corset. If you don't, the lace will hang down instead of out. Pull the lace gently outwards as you attach it.

11 Glue a tiny silk ribbon bow to the top and bottom of the silk panel and an optional silk ribbon rose.

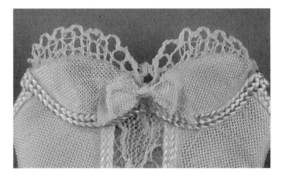

The Bra

1 Cut two lower cups and a section of upper cup scalloped lace as for the corset.

2 Glue these to some flat ⅝in (16mm) lace so just the edge is peeping out at the bottom.

3 When thoroughly dry, turn the bra over and trim the flat lace on the inside of the cups. Turn the bra back to the right side and trim the two outer sides of the bra diagonally from the edge of the cups to the bottom of the bra.

4 Attach the upper cup lace to the lower cups and trim the two outer sides in line with the flat lace.

5 Glue lacet ribbon to the underside of the cups gluing the edges to the inside. Glue lacet ribbon from the lower outer edge of the bra up the sides and leave a 2½in (63mm) strip at the top to later form the straps or, alternatively, gluing the edges under the upper edge for a strapless bra. Glue another piece of lacet from the lower outer edge on one side around the back of the bra to the other side. Finally, glue the straps into position trimming any excess.

6 Add a small optional triangle of lace to the two outer edges to create deeper sides and a tiny bow and rose to the centre of the cups.

The Panties

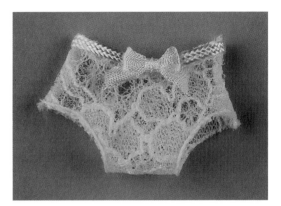

1 Cut out the panties in lace and apply Fray Check. Attach a thread outline around the two leg sections. This is a technique not to be rushed. The thread needs to be glued to the very edge only.

2 Fold the panties in half and with right sides together, apply a little glue to the side seams.

3 Turn to the right side when thoroughly dry and attach some lacet ribbon to the upper edge starting at one side. Add a central bow to the front of the waist.

The Suspenders

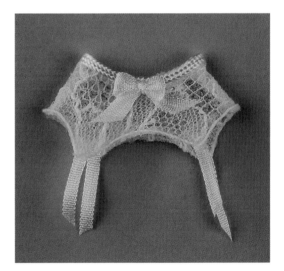

1 Cut two suspender shapes from lace. Fray Check the edges then join the sides with a neatly glued seam.

2 Turn to the right side and attach a thread outline to the entire lower edge of the suspender forming the points. Add a lacet ribbon trim around the upper edge of the suspender and a central bow trim.

3 Attach a piece of $\frac{1}{16}$in (2mm) silk ribbon to each of the four points to hold up the stockings.

The Nightgown

1 Make up the shaped top as for the bra, leaving ³⁄₈in (10mm) deep sides.

2 Apply Fray Check to the skirt and join the back edges with a tiny glued seam. When dry, press and gather the upper edge of the skirt with a small running stitch.

3 Turn under and glue a ¼in (6mm) hem on the lower edge then apply a lace trim to the right side of the gown over the glue line.

4 Pull up the gathers so when laid flat the upper edge of the gown is 1½in (38mm) wide. Press the folds flat to minimize the bulk. Pin and glue the upper edge of the skirt to the inside of the shaped top, trimming the lace sides and gluing the back edge.

5 Add ¹⁄₁₆in (2mm) silk ribbon straps and a bow and tails trim to the centre front.

Parasols, Purses and Pumps

Three styles of purse, a parasol and a pair of ballet pumps are included in this section. There are also some tips for painting shoes on your miniature dolls and adding trims.

Parasol

I have used a 5in (127mm) length of thin dowel to make the centre of a parasol. Alternatively, you can use a shaped cocktail stick. Both need to be painted in a silver, gold or ivory acrylic paint.

1 Glue the edge of a piece of ³⁄₁₆in (4mm) silk ribbon ¼in (6mm) up from the bottom, after sewing one edge to a point, at an angle, or attach two ribbons in coordinating colours with a slight overlap, as shown below on the 'Royal Ascot' parasol. Wind the ribbon up the stick and finish about 1in (25mm) from the top.

2 Gather a little lace for the base of the ribbon and either gather a longer piece for the top or add some ruffles by sewing a gathering line up the centre of some ¼in (7mm) ribbon.

3 Complete the parasol with an optional tiny tassel hanging on a thread and glued to the top of the stick. Add a ribbon rosette, rose and tails.

Purses

The first two styles do not open but the third does if you would like to add some miniature items for the bride. The really fun part is adding the decoration and coordinating them to complement a gown. They also make an attractive display for a miniature salon.

Style 1

The wrap-around style is the easiest to create and it can be made from either leather, suede or silk. If you prefer to use leather or suede they will need to be very fine. I can recommend miniature teddy bear suede, which is available in a huge range of colours.

1 Cut the shape in your chosen material using the wrap-over template on page 186. For the silk version, cut the fabric ⅛in (3mm) bigger on the two sides and the upper edge.

2 Fold in and glue ¹⁄₁₆in (1.5mm) on all sides, cutting the smallest tip from each corner diagonally for a neat corner. This is not necessary for suede or leather purses.

3 Cut a small piece of card to fit within the finished space.

4 Decide upon a handle, this can either be fine chain or a filigree finding with some bunka and ribbon. Fold the purse in half and then glue it together with the handle sandwiched within.

5 Decorate the upper edges with a little lace, a bow and a rose.

Style 2

For this simple yet effective style you will need some silk, white acrylic paint, $\frac{1}{16}$in (2mm) silk ribbon in several shades for the roses, $\frac{3}{4}$in (19mm) length of $\frac{1}{2}$in (13mm) dowel, thin card, paper or velvet leaves, a small length of optional $\frac{1}{4}$in pleated lace and an optional tiny filigree clasp.

1 Cut a $\frac{1}{4}$in (6mm) strip of card for the faux lid and a $\frac{1}{2}$in (13mm) strip for the faux base, just long enough to reach around the circumference of the dowel.

2 Cut two pieces of silk $\frac{1}{4}$in (6mm) deeper and $\frac{3}{8}$in (10mm) longer than the strips of card and two circles of silk with a diameter of $\frac{3}{4}$in (19mm) . Apply Fray Check fabric sealant to the four pieces.

3 Place the card on the silk with a $\frac{1}{8}$in (3mm) space on the left-hand side and the top and bottom and a $\frac{1}{4}$in (6mm) space on the right-hand side. Fold over and glue the left side of the silk onto the card. Fold and glue the right side of the silk up to the edge of the card then fold the top and bottom over the card. Repeat for the second strip.

4 Paint the two ends of the dowel with acrylic and leave to dry. Glue one end of the dowel to the centre of a circle of silk. Cut the border around the dowel with tiny snips from the outer edge inwards to $\frac{1}{32}$in (about 1mm) from the actual dowel. Fold and glue the tabs down over the side of the dowel as neatly as possible. Repeat at the other end.

5 Glue a ¼in (6mm) strip of silk with no overlap around the dowel where the base and the lid meet. Glue the base of the purse level with the bottom edge of the dowel and overlap the fabric end over the card end. Repeat for the lid.

6 Thread the ends of the lace pleats and form into a neat circle, stitching the join with a few overcast stitches. Glue to the top of the purse and add a small arrangement of silk roses and leaves.

7 Make a handle from a length of silk with all edges glued firmly over and attach to the purse then add the clasp.

Style 3

This dolly purse is made from silk with a sturdy silk-covered card base. The sides are soft and the purse can be filled with a little wadding or small accessories to give it a nice rounded shape. Trim the purse with pretty bows and roses.

1 Cut out a circle of card with a diameter of ⅝in (16mm) and a circle of silk with a diameter of ⅞in (22mm). Add Fray Check to the silk and, when dry, glue the card circle to the centre.

2 Make tiny snips in the silk from the outside of the circle to the card then fold over and glue the tabs to the underside of the card.

3 Cut a rectangle of silk 2¾ x 1¼in (32 x 70mm) and apply Fray Check to all edges. Turn under and glue a ⅛in (3mm) hem along one side for the top of the bag. Sew a row of gathering stitches along the other long side, ⅛in (3mm) from the edge and another row ¼in (6mm) down from the top edge of the purse below the hem line.

4 With right sides together, fold the rectangle in half and close the back seam. Press and turn to the right side.

5 Pull the gathering thread gently at the bottom of the purse and arrange the gathers evenly before gluing them around the edge of the card base to the side with the glued tabs.

6 Pull the gathers at the top of the purse and tie off the thread. Add a small ¹⁄₁₆in (2mm) silk ribbon handle to the inside of the purse and trim with ribbons and roses.

Ballet Pumps

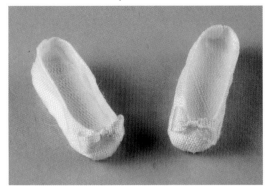

1 To make the bridal ballerina pumps, trace the five pattern pieces on page 186, cut them out in silk and add Fray Check fabric sealant to all the edges with a fine paintbrush.

2 Cut out the Vilene toe cap and position it ½in (13mm) down from the neckline of the slipper and iron it on. Clip the inner front curves of the neckline to the Vilene, taking care not to cut past the Fray Check, fold down the clipped curves and glue them evenly to the Vilene. Turn down and press ½in (13mm) hem around the entire slipper neckline and glue into place.

3 Join the back of the slipper with a ⅛in (3mm) seam and press the seam open. Turn down the hem and glue it into place on the back seam.

4 Run a tiny gathering stitch around the lower edge of the slipper where the sole is to be attached. Pull the thread fairly tightly and then shape it with your fingertips using a modelling tool as a former to shape the slipper. Fasten off the thread. Attach the upper to the sole using the modelling tool to shape the toe then press the sole into position.

5 Make an insole for your shoe by gluing a piece of the silk to some thin card. Leave this to dry before cutting out the insole using the pattern piece. Glue the insole into the slipper and add two optional ribbon ties and finally the silk roses to the tiny toes. You can also decorate the front of the bridal slippers with a tiny piece of pleated lace and a buckle or tiny bows with a seed pearl stitched to the centre. You can give the slippers a dusting of glitter too, a spray with the glitter mist hairspray, or add a few tiny Swarovski crystals to the front on top of a circle of ¹⁄₁₆in (1.5mm) lace edging.

Painting Slippers on Your Doll

Paint shoe outlines with acrylic paint directly onto your dolls and either leave them with this finish or add some PVA to the dry acrylic before dusting it with glitter dust. You can then trim them with tiny silk ribbon bows and roses. Remember, always paint shoes on a doll before fitting her gown.

Fans

A simple fan decorated with colour-coordinating trims such as bows, roses and small feathers provide the perfect elegant accessory.

This is a simple paper fan that can be decorated with lace and other pretty embellishements to look really speacial.

To make the feather fan pictured below you will need two small half circles of card with a ½in (13mm) lower edge and some marabou feathers.

1 Cut the tips from some marabou feathers to a length of 1in (25mm).

2 Trim the feathery strands so that you are left with the firmer part of the feather tips. Glue these around the upper round edge and sandwich them with the second half circle.

3 Add some lace, a ribbon bow and silk roses for trims.

1 Score and fold a narrow strip of paper measuring 6 x ¾in (152 x 19mm). The fold lines need to be ³⁄₁₆in (5mm) apart.

2 Open out the card and glue some narrow lace along the upper edge of the fan then glue the lower edge of each fold firmly together.

3 Decorate with small roses, leaves and a bow.

Designer Collections

Crystal Snowflake

The lovely set includes a tiara which has three central silver maple leaves sprinkled with Swarovski crystals, a Venetian mask, which has a row of the leaves across the brow sprinkled with crystals, and a necklace with a central maple leaf pendant and a few more crystals. The mask has strands of curled marabou feathers glued at the base for a beautiful finishing touch.

Venetian Rhapsody

A Venetian mask with a gold trim is perfect with the gown featured on page 94.

Ocean Dreams

This set comprises a necklace with a little aqua glitter dust, pearls and tiny seashells, and a 'wand' made from a mask stick decorated with glitter dust and tiny stars.

Hollywood Panache

A Style 2 necklace (see page 139) with ruby glitter dust and a central ruby crystal complement the striking ruby silk gown.

Here are some accessories which I created to go with a selection of the gowns presented earlier.
I hope they will inspire you to create your own unique range of matching accessories.

Royal Ascot

A parasol, pill-box hat, purse and choker create the ideal accessories for the dress inspired by Royal Ascot.

Pumpkins and Butterflies

This set includes a tiara with central pearly pink baby teardrop leaves, a little fine pink glitter dust and a butterfly. The Venetian mask has pearl-trimmed eyelets, tiny pearly teardrops at the centre of the brow with another butterfly and some pink glitter dust. There is a ribbon choker, also with a butterfly. A matching trimmed horseshoe completes the accessory set.

Blue Moon

As well as a blue corset and beaded bouquet, the Venetian mask has blue glitter dust across the brow and down the stick, blue curled feathers and a pretty blue tassel.

151

Good Luck Charms

Wearing something blue has long been considered lucky for the bride and it has become a tradition for brides to wear a blue-trimmed garter for this reason. In earlier times there existed the tradition of throwing a bridal garter to the male guests; the one to catch it would be the next to marry. Later, the throwing of a bouquet was introduced to please the female guests.

Garters

To make a lace-trimmed garter:

1 Insert some ¹⁄₁₆in (2mm) blue silk ribbon through some ¹⁄₄in (6mm) insertion lace.

2 Pull the ribbon gathers, glue the edge to the lace and trim. Sew the back seam.

3 Trim with a little blue bow and an optional small rose.

Horseshoes

I've used commercially available horseshoes which, although only available in a silver colour, can be made to have a gold effect by using some liquid gold leaf.

1 Cut a 2in (51mm) length of ¹⁄₁₆in (2mm) silk ribbon in your chosen colour and glue the edges to the underside of the horseshoe to form a carry handle.

2 Gather a small length of ¹⁄₈in (3mm) lace trim cut from a wider lace trim and glue evenly around the horseshoe. When gluing the edges of the lace into position, taper and trim them diagonally into the ribbon carry handle.

3 Trim the lower centre of the horseshoe with a tiny bow, silk rose or a themed trim.

Rings and Ring Pillow

The ring pillow is for the presentation of the precious wedding rings. Make a beautiful yet simple ring pillow with a small 1½in (38mm) square of waffle silk cut on the bias so the tiny squares are diagonal on the surface of the pillow and a 1½in (38mm) square of plain silk for the back of the pillow. To make a tiny wedding ring I buy an inexpensive gold necklace with round links that I can take apart. Interestingly, the 'ring finger' became so because it was once thought that a vein in that finger ran directly to the heart.

1 With right sides together, sew a ⅛in (3mm) seam leaving a gap for turning.

2 Turn through and lightly press the seams only on the plain side of the pillow.

3 Add a little wadding and sew up the gap.

4 Gather some ⅛in (3mm) lace edging, again cut from a deeper lace and attach it evenly around the edge of the pillow.

5 Cut two tiny links and thread them onto two small loops of 1/16in (2mm) silk ribbon.

6 Glue the edges of the ribbon to one corner of the pillow.

7 Add a tiny perfectly formed silk ribbon bow to the top edge of the ring ribbon loops.

Confetti and Favours

The throwing of confetti originates from the custom of throwing grain or rice, which are both 'life-giving' seeds and would therefore bestow fertility on the happy couple. Favours are not symbolic in the same way; they are simply given to the guests as thank you gifts. You could fill a flower-girl basket with several of these to be handed out at the reception.

Confetti

To make the little confetti box shown here, copy the template on page 186 onto your choice of floral paper and fold as indicated. Alternatively, you could make up tiny cones and fill them with small pieces of confetti then place them in a ribbon and flower-trimmed basket for a flower girl or bridesmaid.

Favours

1 Fold a 2in (51mm) length of ⅜in (10mm) Ruban Mousseline organza ribbon in half and press. Turn in ¼in (6mm) on the two narrow edges and press.

2 Oversew the two sides of the bag from just above the fold to the corners. Fill with your five favours.

3 Sew a tiny row of running stitches through all layers between the top stitch at each side as shown. Pull gently and fasten off. Finally, add a miniature silk ribbon bow and rose to the front of the gathers.

Alternatively:

1 Cut circles of tulle with a diameter of 1–1¼in (25–32mm) and sew a row of running stitches all the way round ³⁄₁₆in (5mm) from the outer edge.

2 Place five polymer clay almonds in the centre and draw up the stitches before fastening off. Add a tiny silk ribbon bow and rose or a tiny parchment flower.

The Cake

The wedding cake is eaten to bestow good luck and fertility. The tradition is that the couple cut it together to cement their union and the sharing of a future life together. The cake usually takes centre stage at the reception on a beautifully dressed table.

1 Make a polymer clay wedding cake and cut a base from ⅛in (3mm) wood or thick card which is ³⁄₁₆in (5mm) bigger than the cake all the way around.

2 Round off the upper edge of the wood base and paint with silver or acrylic paint.

3 Glue some ¼in (7mm) silk ribbon around the base of the cake and make a small floral arrangement. This can be designed to match a bouquet, urns or a floral table display. A tiny swag of ivy glued to the sides of the cake provides a lovely decoration. You can sit further tiers on top of the base, placing the floral arrangement on top.

Tip

The cake illustrated above was baked inside the cutter. Leave the cake until almost cool before removing it. If you find a crack in the polymer clay, carefully push the clay cake out of the cutter and clamp tightly until cool. Leave the clamps in place for a few hours.

4 Dress the side drop of a table with some box-pleated fine cotton lawn.

5 Cut a strip of silk tulle 8in (203mm) deep multiplied by the circumference of the table plus ½in (13mm) and turn under the top 2in (51mm).

6 Sew six gathering lines down the length of tulle at regular intervals, keeping the hem in place with the end stitches. Pull the gathers and fasten off.

7 Attach the upper-hemmed edge to the edge of the table with a little glue, pulling the drapes gently into place.

8 Add a silk ribbon bow to the top of the gathers and an optional rose.

9 Complete the table with a silver cake knife with a silk ribbon-tied bow around the handle and some champagne flutes.

Floral Arrangements

Floral arrangements in miniature always look best if formed with the tiniest, daintiest flowers whilst allowing light to show through, rather than having a solid mass of flowers.

Waterfall Bouquet

A traditional waterfall bouquet illustrates a showering effect of flowers on a background of pretty and spacious foliage. It has two or three main flowers in the centre and the remaining flowers are very small. This attention to space needs to be refined further if you are to create a similar bouquet in miniature. Instead of simply reducing each flower down to the correct scale, you also need to think of the overall effect of the arrangement. It is so important to keep the slightly larger blooms to a bare minimum, just two or three. Surround these with a few much smaller flowers and add some tiny ivy sprigs or babies' breath sprays. To make up a waterfall bouquet you will need:

- ♥ *thin green cake wire*
- ♥ *florists' tape*
- ♥ *long ivy trails or similar foliage*
- ♥ *a selection of buds and full blooms; I have chosen roses and daisies, you could also insert some beaded loops (thread some tiny glass beads onto wire and form into a loop twisting the two ends together)*
- ♥ *a selection of leaves, I have used birch leaves and 'squiggles', which look like an angled 'S' shape*
- ♥ *spray gloss for paper craft*
- ♥ *silk ribbon*
- ♥ *a few sprigs of lavender.*

1 Begin with one trail of ivy, the length you want the bouquet to be. Spray with a gloss finish. Twist a tiny rosebud onto the stem ¾in (about 20mm) of the way down and another just above it. Add two lavender sprigs, a birch leaf sprig and a 'squiggle' leaf sprig.

2 Make up three individual arrangements, each including a lavender and ivy sprig and a rose. Trim the wires back, leaving the ivy wire long, and cover with florists' tape. You should have only one wire at the top now. Make another sprig of birch leaves. Begin attaching the four sprigs.

3 Make up three medium-length trails of ivy and attach them to the first trails in stepped positions so that the twists are not all in the same place. Twist further rosebuds onto the trails again so they are not level with other rosebuds.

4 Join on some daisies and rosebuds as fillers. This is where you could insert beaded loops.

5 Trim the wires back and secure with glue and tape. Form the edge of the wires into a little hook shape, bind with tape and add a silk ribbon bow and tails.

Posies

These are small spherical-shaped flower arrangements with a Victorian influence.

The bride in Victorian times would carry a 'Tussie Mussie'. This was a long narrow vase with a silver cone-shaped filigree banding around it. Water in the bottom of the vase kept the flowers fresh throughout the proceedings. The flowers would often have ribbons and sometimes a lace collar. To create small posies use three central roses surrounded by smaller flowers and foliage.

1 Pleat some ½in (13mm) lace and place around the arrangement to check for sizing.

2 Trim the lace allowing for a 1/16in (1.5mm) overlap, thread a needle and thread through the very edge of the pleat before placing it around the flowers.

3 Gently pull the gathers and fasten off.

4 Keep the lace collar in place with a little glue at the base and glue the join.

5 Add a silk or organza bow and tails.

Buttonholes

Create a buttonhole with a single medium rose and a daisy to match the overall theme. Add optional leaves, either in gold or silver or traditional green, behind them. Fasten with a 1/16in (2mm) silk ribbon bow and short tails.

Flower Baskets

Young bridesmaids and flower girls often carry a small basket with a long handle that can be filled in various ways, such as with rose petals which are then scattered in the aisle for the bride to walk upon.

1 Glue a small dome of oasis with a base diameter of ¾in (about 20mm) to the centre of a basket which has been edged with pleated lace and the handle trimmed with a swirl of ribbon.

2 Glue some rosebuds and ivy at each side, reaching to the edge of the basket.

3 Gradually build up the stems and foliage around the basket edge and place three larger blooms in a triangle at the top with a medium bloom at the centre of them.

4 Insert a few medium-size blooms or daisies as fillers around the sides with a scattering of rosebuds and some foliage.

Various other floral-themed items carried by young bridesmaids and flower girls include a pomander, made from a small sphere of flowers pressed into a ball of oasis and carried on a length of ribbon; twisted cones of confetti to be handed to the guests as they leave the church; garlands of tulle and ribbon-tied favours, a ribbon-bound hoop with garlands of flowers twisted around it, or simply flowers.

Decorative Urns

Fill a decorative urn for adding drama to
a reception setting. These urns can also be used
for other settings – I placed some in my Salon.

1 Starting at the back, place the taller foliage and
plants. I have used brass leaves and lavender.
Two or three very large waterlilies of different
heights were placed at the centre front along with
medium-size roses in pink and buttermilk.

2 Fill in the spaces with full-bloom roses and
some small daisies.

3 Finally, add a few ivy trails to the front of the
arrangement.

Floral Table Display

1 Glue a dome of oasis to a small, clear, cake stand.

2 Fill in the flowers and foliage in exactly the same way as the flower girls' basket on page 161.

3 Slightly extend the ivy sprigs at the sides so that they point down towards the table.

Column-Based Floral Arrangements

Make a free-standing arrangement with a decorative column to stand by your wedding table. For this arrangement I have used taller lavender sprigs for the back, some larger lillies for the centre front, seven medium blooms in two shades and some daisies for fillers and ivy trails at the front. Two rosebuds and some short ivy stems form the arms and a bow and tails complete the arrangement.

Patterns and Templates

Patterns and templates are shown actual size unless marked otherwise

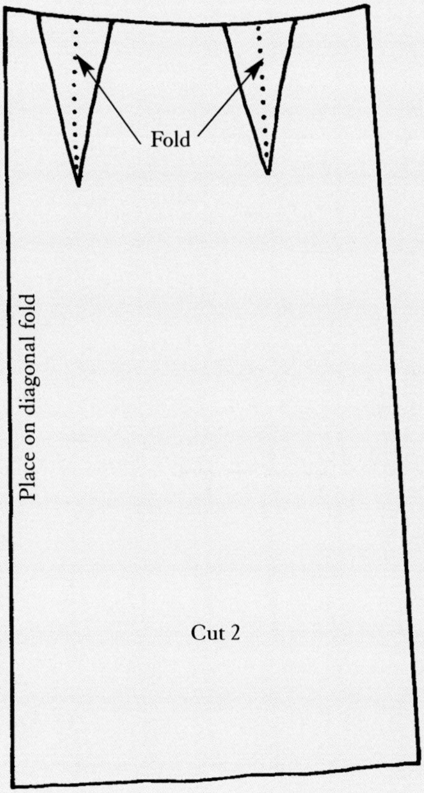

Bodice A

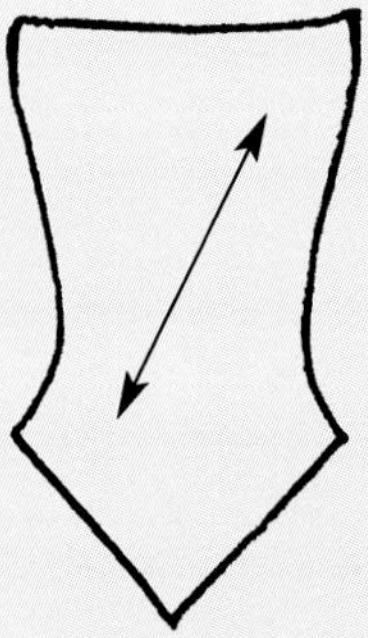

'V' lower front
straight neckline
Cut 1

Gathering line

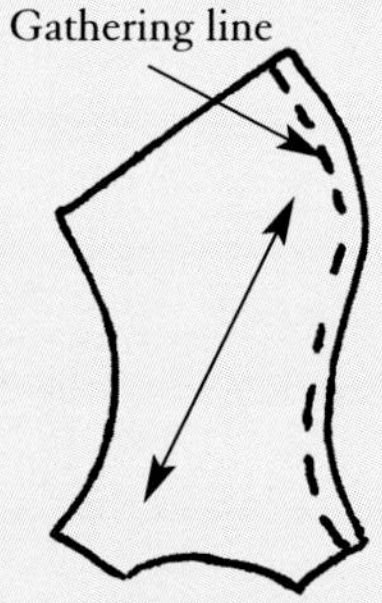

Bodice side
Cut 2, 1 in reverse

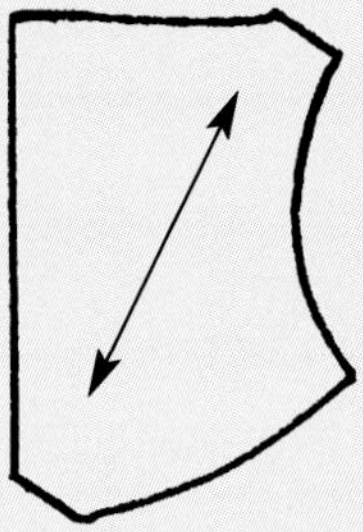

Dipped lower back
Cut 2, 1 in reverse

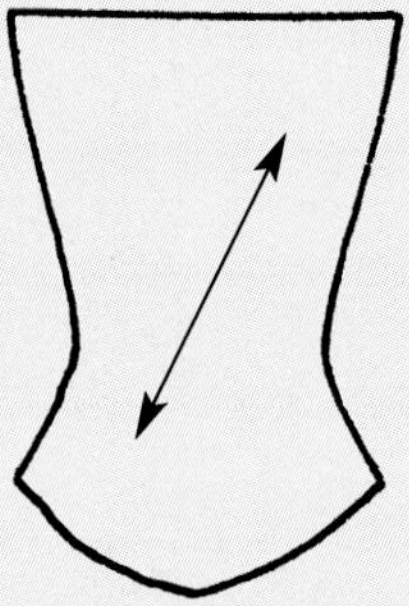

Dipped lower front
straight neckline
Cut 1

Snip here

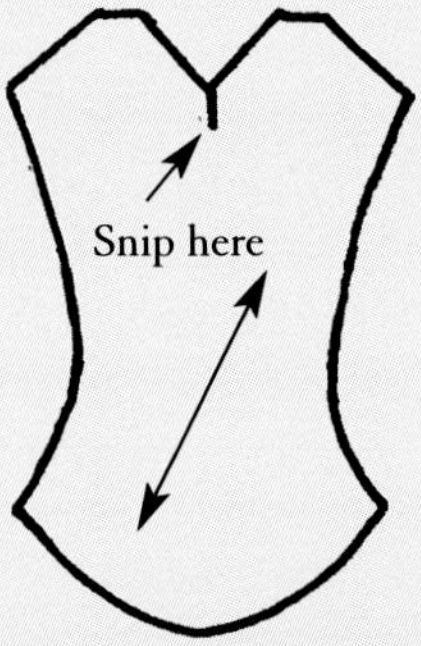

Dipped lower front
sweetheart neckline

Snip here

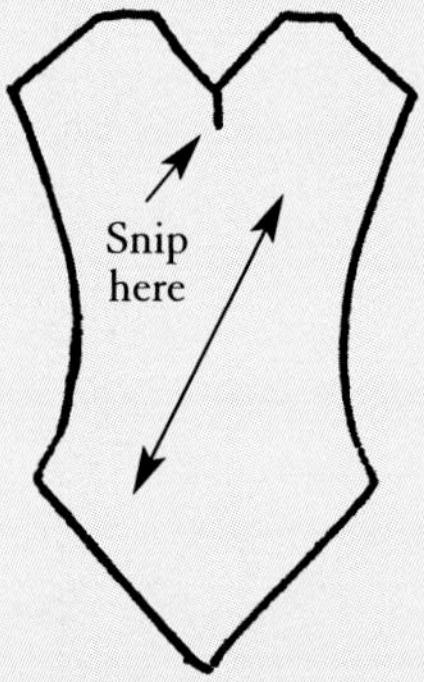

'V' lower front
sweetheart neckline

Petticoat

Fold

Place on diagonal fold

Cut 2

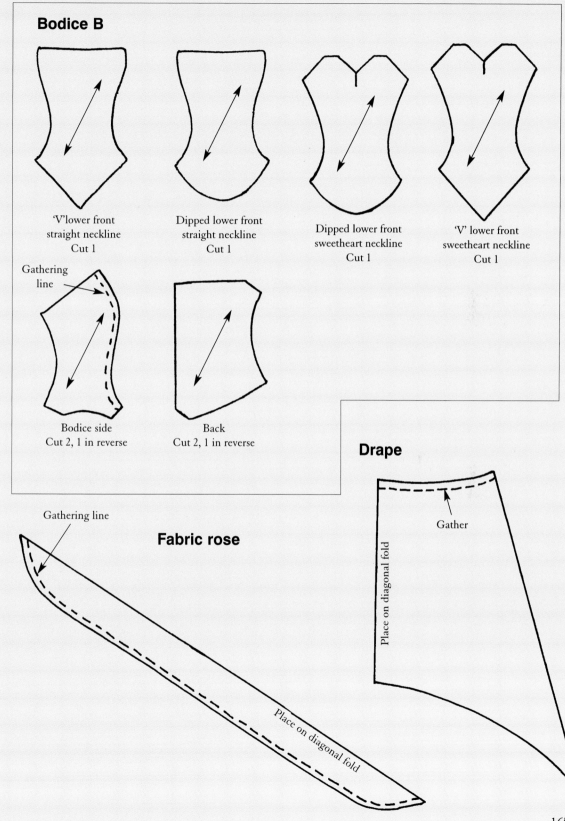

Bodice B

'V' lower front
straight neckline
Cut 1

Dipped lower front
straight neckline
Cut 1

Dipped lower front
sweetheart neckline
Cut 1

'V' lower front
sweetheart neckline
Cut 1

Gathering
line

Bodice side
Cut 2, 1 in reverse

Back
Cut 2, 1 in reverse

Drape

Gather

Place on diagonal fold

Gathering line

Fabric rose

Place on diagonal fold

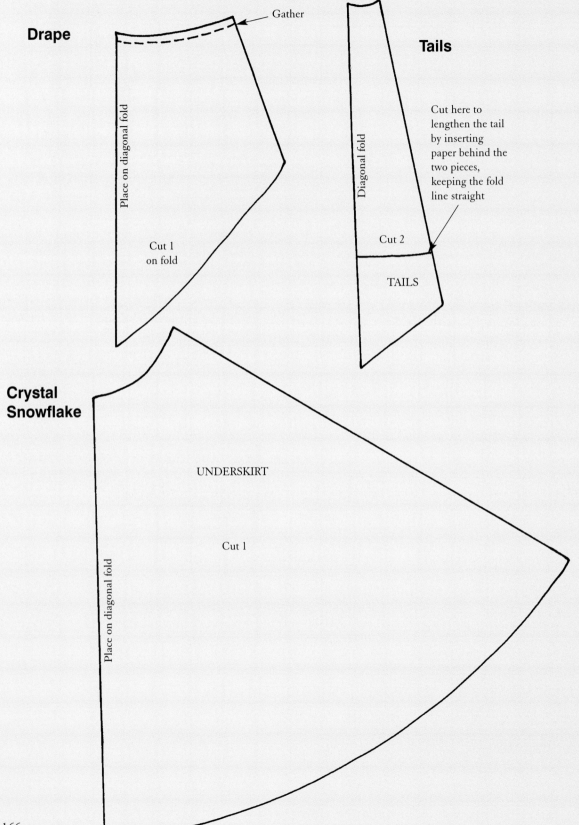

Drape

Gather

Place on diagonal fold

Cut 1
on fold

Tails

Diagonal fold

Cut here to
lengthen the tail
by inserting
paper behind the
two pieces,
keeping the fold
line straight

Cut 2

TAILS

**Crystal
Snowflake**

UNDERSKIRT

Cut 1

Place on diagonal fold

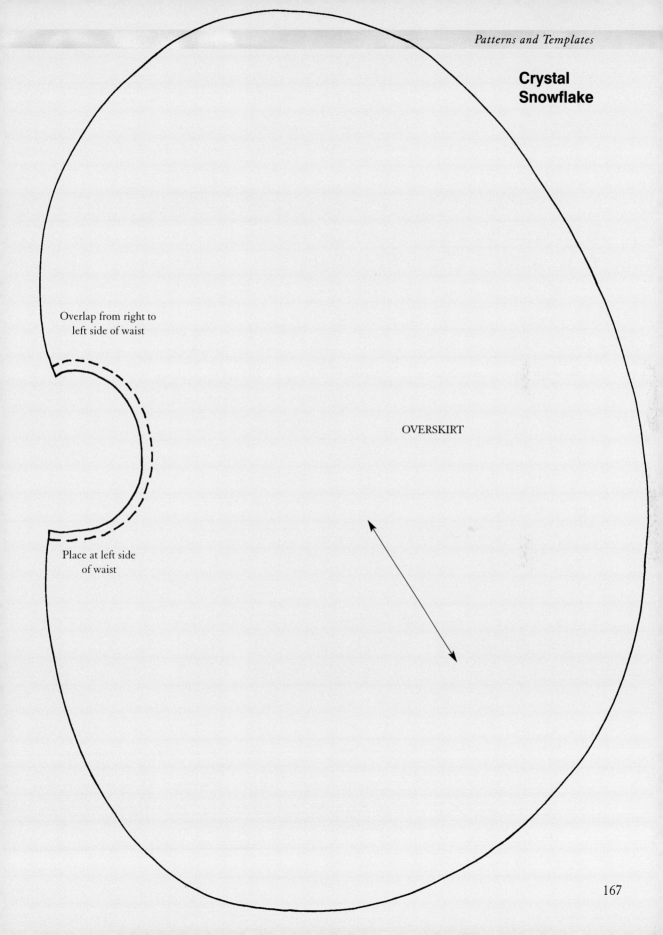

**Crystal
Snowflake**

Overlap from right to
left side of waist

OVERSKIRT

Place at left side
of waist

167

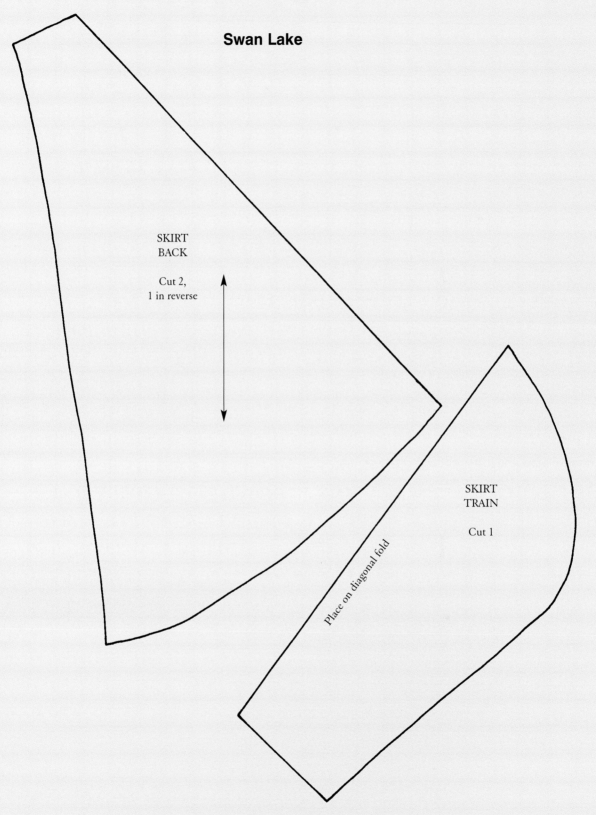

Swan Lake

SKIRT
BACK

Cut 2,
1 in reverse

SKIRT
TRAIN

Cut 1

Place on diagonal fold

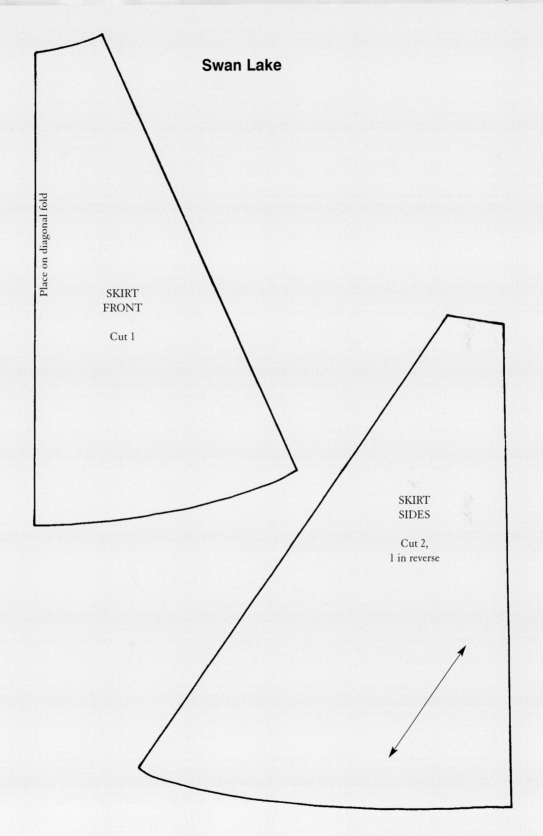

Swan Lake

Place on diagonal fold

SKIRT
FRONT

Cut 1

SKIRT
SIDES

Cut 2,
1 in reverse

La Dolce Vita

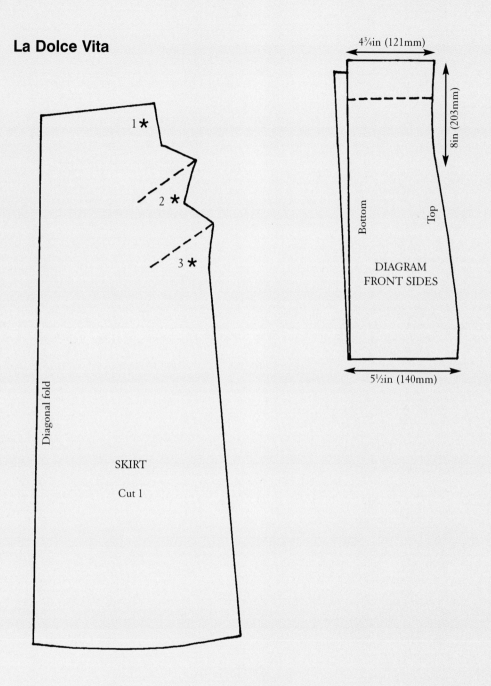

1 ★

2 ★

3 ★

Diagonal fold

SKIRT

Cut 1

4¾in (121mm)

8in (203mm)

Bottom

Top

DIAGRAM
FRONT SIDES

5½in (140mm)

Venetian Rhapsody

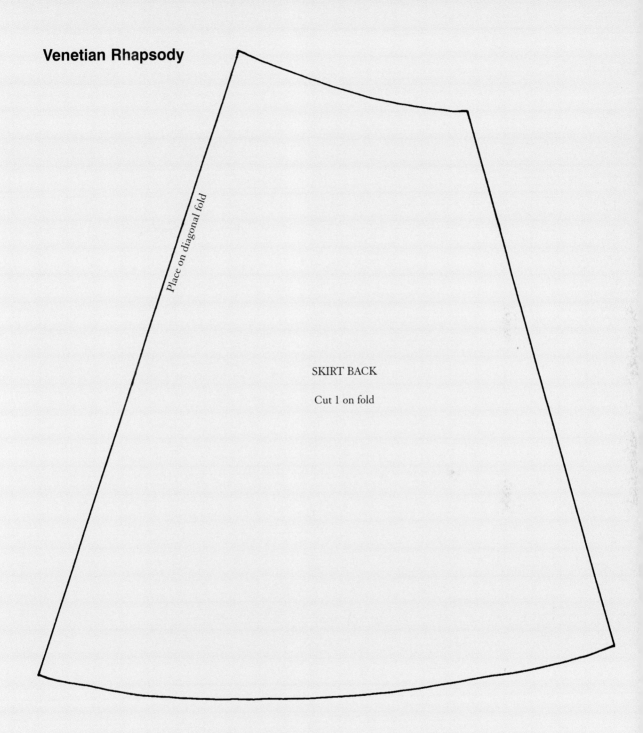

Place on diagonal fold

SKIRT BACK

Cut 1 on fold

Venetian Rhapsody

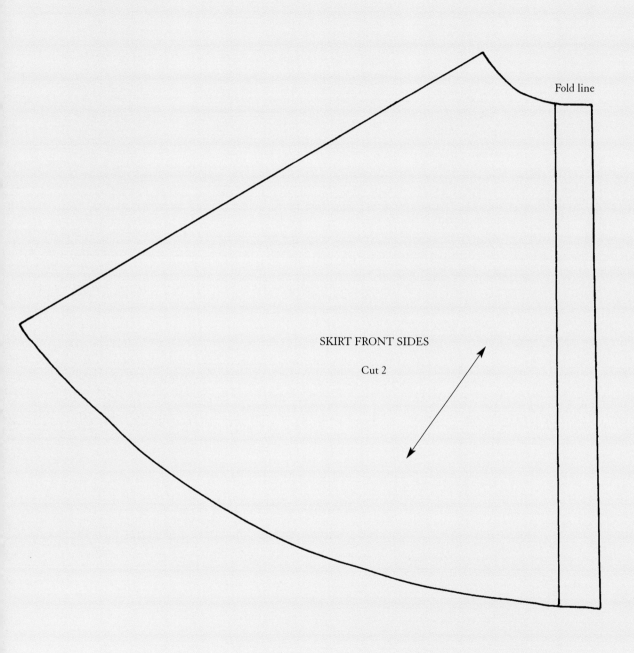

Fold line

SKIRT FRONT SIDES

Cut 2

Venetian Rhapsody

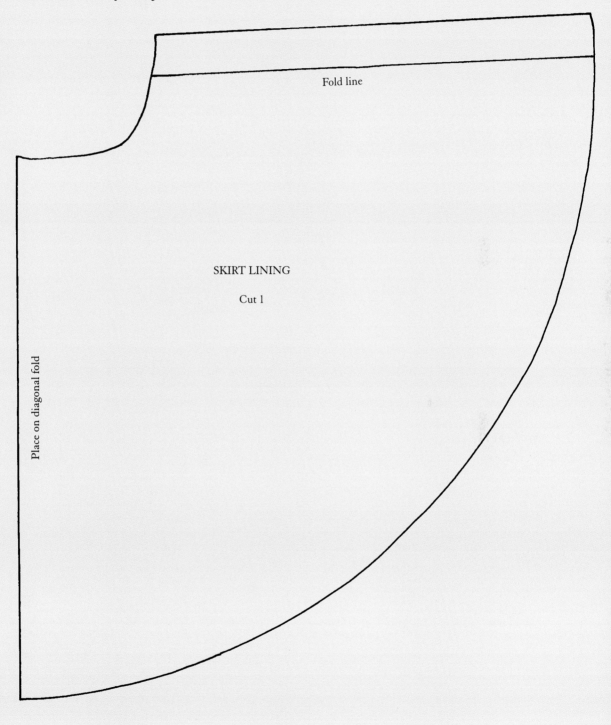

Fold line

SKIRT LINING

Cut 1

Place on diagonal fold

Royal Ascot

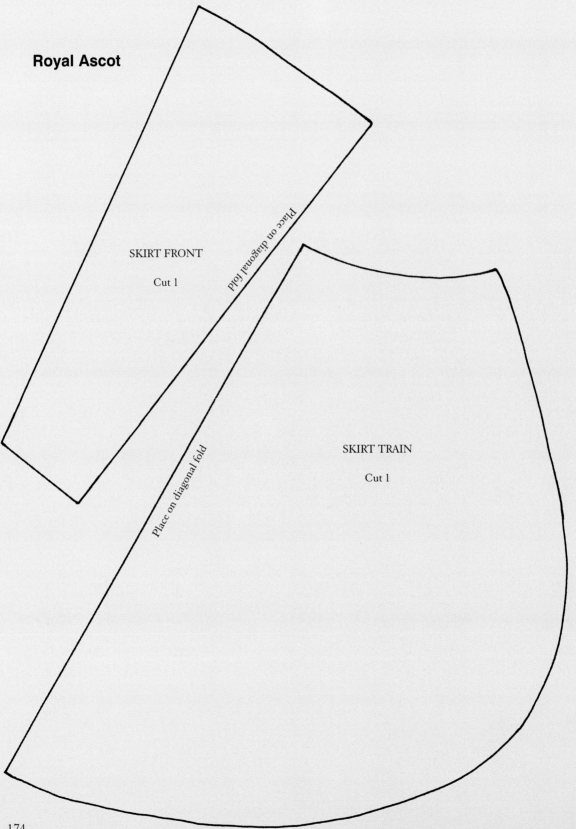

SKIRT FRONT

Cut 1

Place on diagonal fold

Place on diagonal fold

SKIRT TRAIN

Cut 1

Royal Ascot

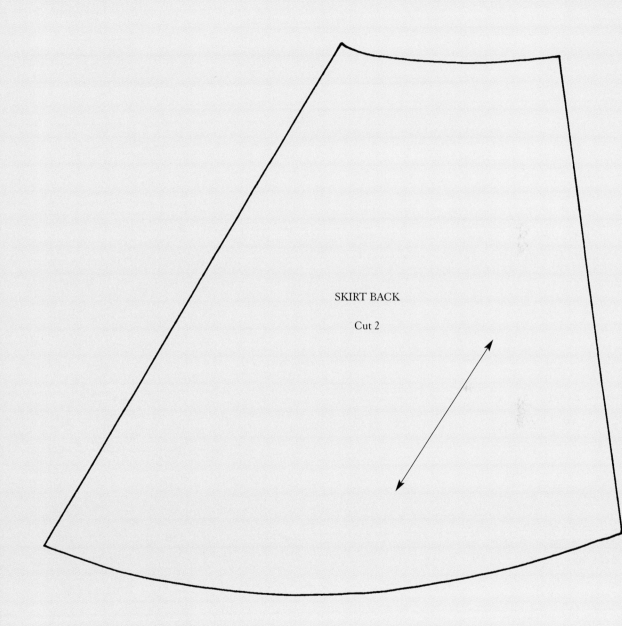

SKIRT BACK

Cut 2

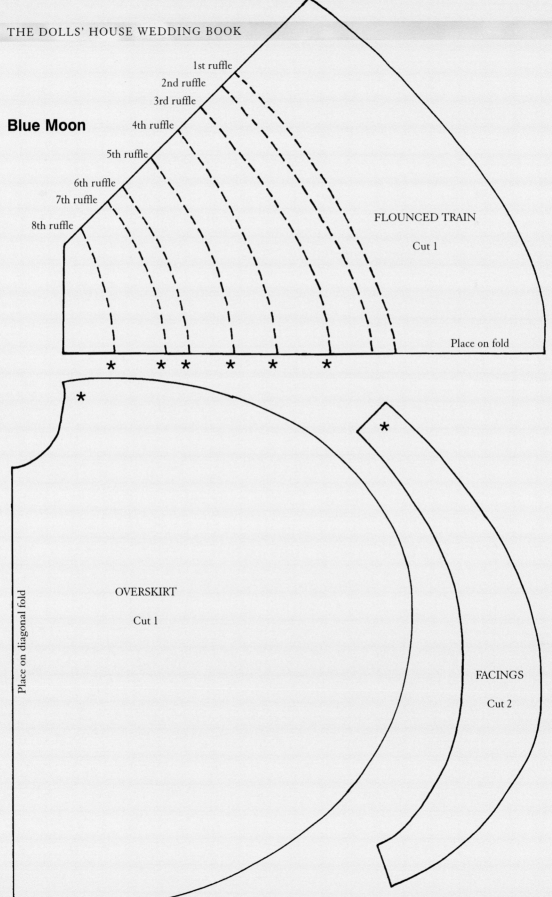

Blue Moon

1st ruffle
2nd ruffle
3rd ruffle
4th ruffle
5th ruffle
6th ruffle
7th ruffle
8th ruffle

FLOUNCED TRAIN

Cut 1

Place on fold

*   * *   *   *   *

*

OVERSKIRT

Cut 1

Place on diagonal fold

*

FACINGS

Cut 2

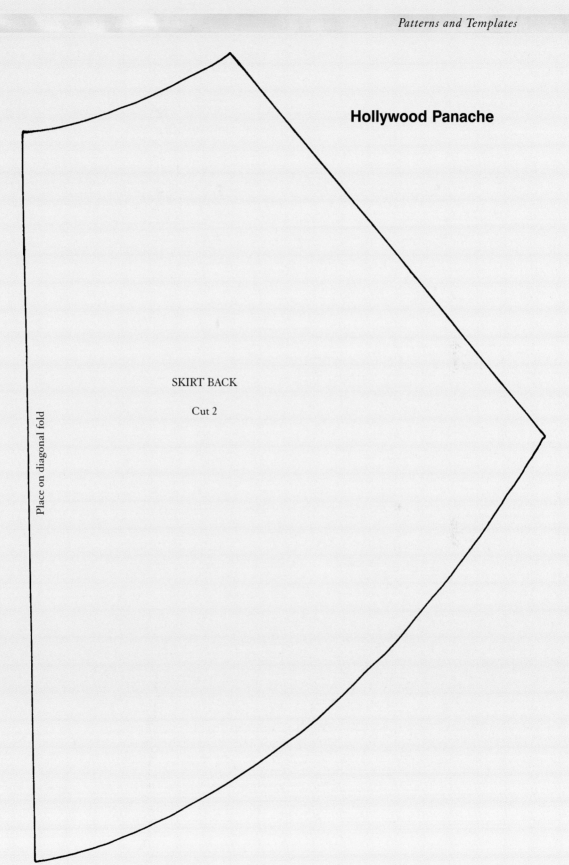

Hollywood Panache

SKIRT BACK

Cut 2

Place on diagonal fold

Hollywood Panache

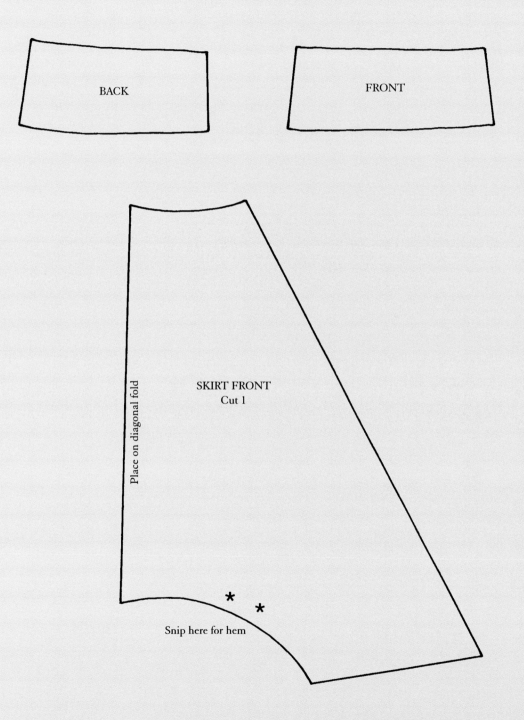

BACK

FRONT

SKIRT FRONT
Cut 1

Place on diagonal fold

*   *

Snip here for hem

A Taste of Honey

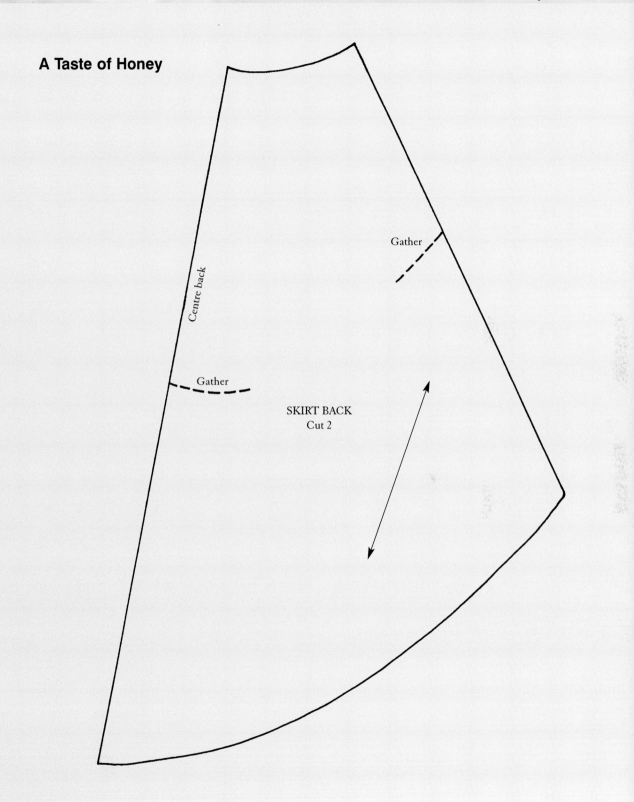

Centre back

Gather

Gather

SKIRT BACK
Cut 2

A Taste of Honey

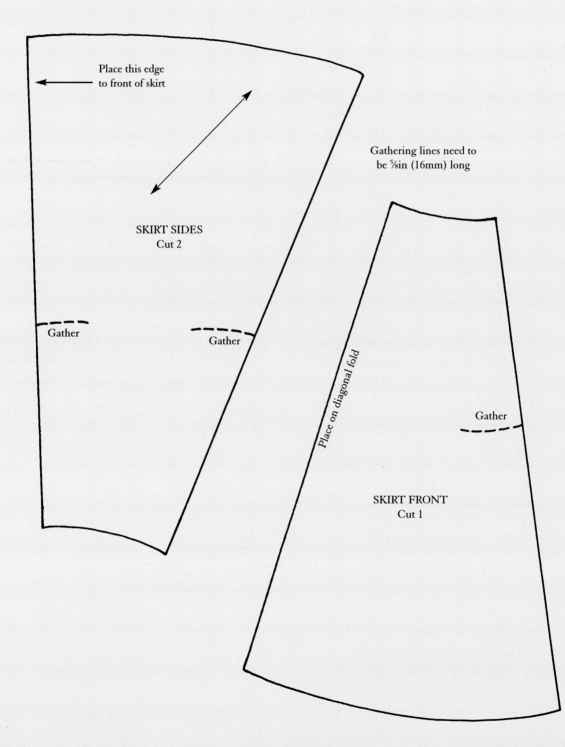

Place this edge
to front of skirt

SKIRT SIDES
Cut 2

Gather

Gather

Gathering lines need to
be ⅝in (16mm) long

Place on diagonal fold

Gather

SKIRT FRONT
Cut 1

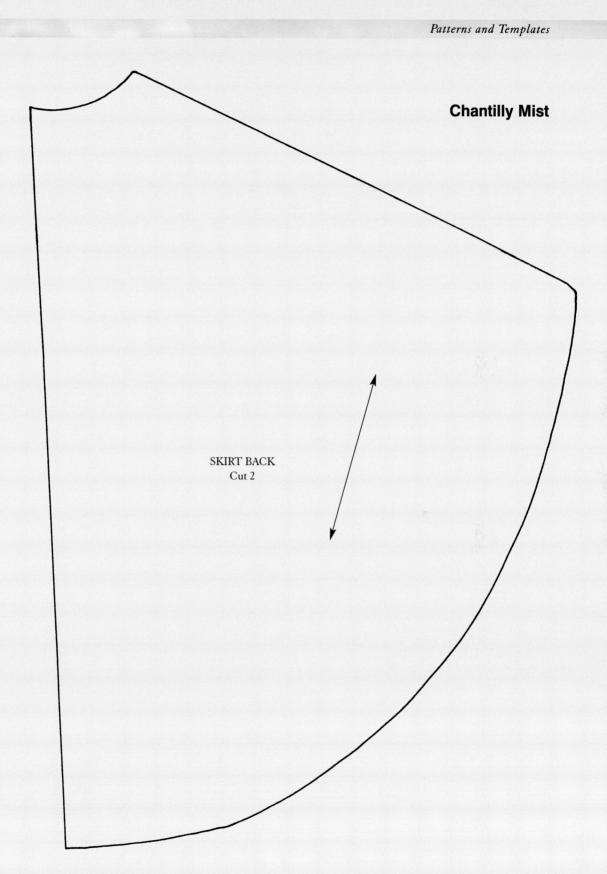

Chantilly Mist

SKIRT BACK
Cut 2

Chantilly Mist

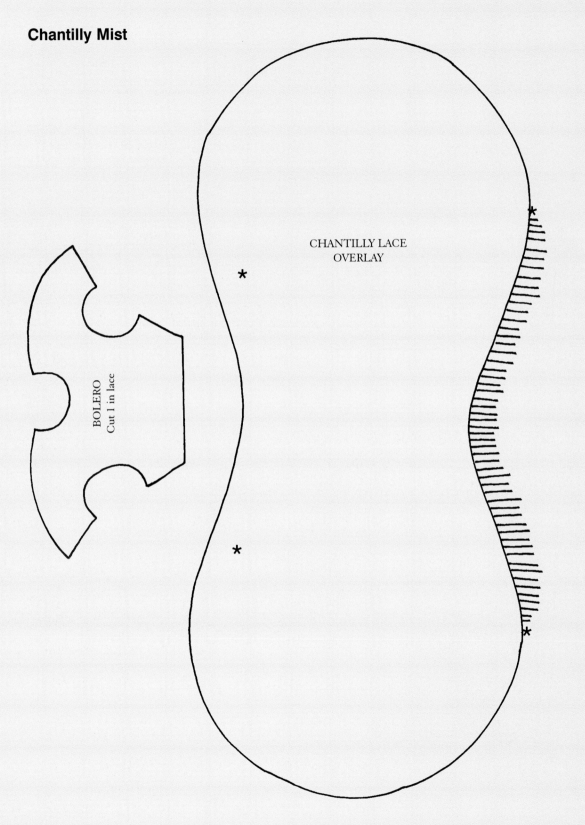

CHANTILLY LACE
OVERLAY

BOLERO
Cut 1 in lace

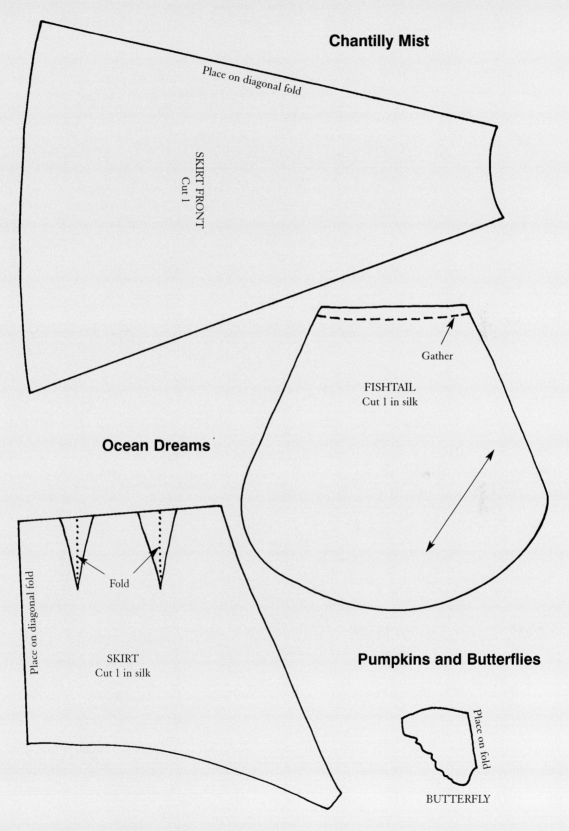

Chantilly Mist

Place on diagonal fold

SKIRT FRONT
Cut 1

Gather

FISHTAIL
Cut 1 in silk

Ocean Dreams

Place on diagonal fold

Fold

SKIRT
Cut 1 in silk

Pumpkins and Butterflies

Place on fold

BUTTERFLY

The patterns for Cascade, No Sew and Dragonfly veils are not shown actual size. Enlarge to the correct size by photocopying them at 200%

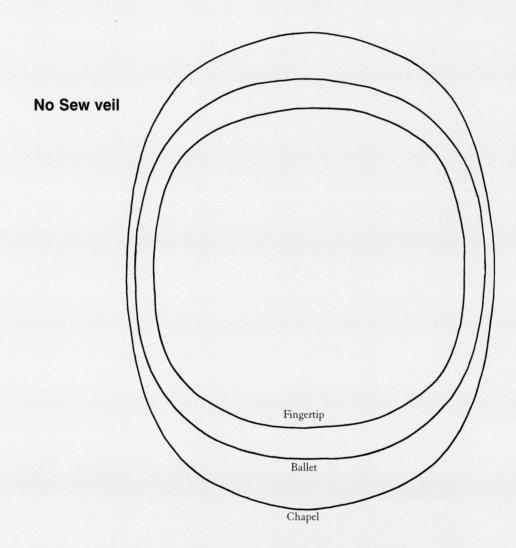

No Sew veil

Fingertip

Ballet

Chapel

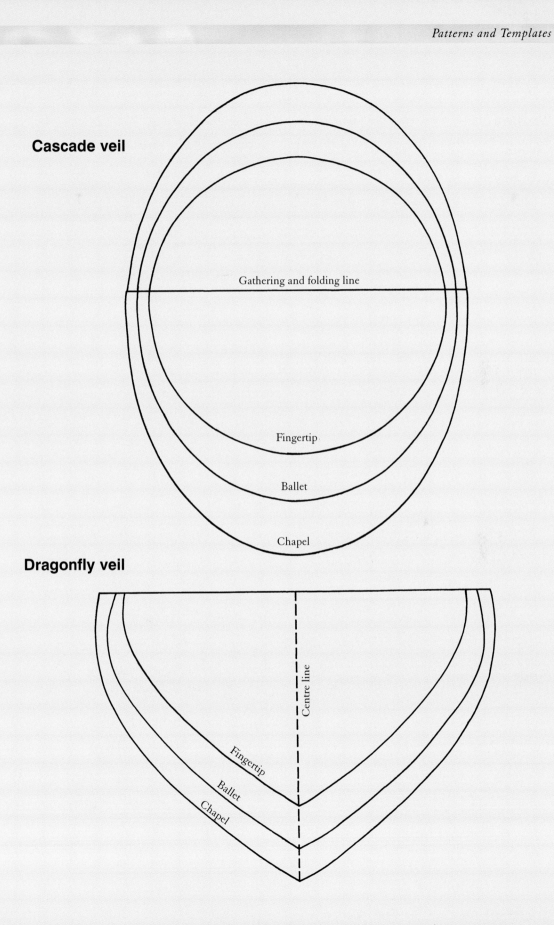

Cascade veil

Gathering and folding line

Fingertip

Ballet

Chapel

Dragonfly veil

Centre line

Fingertip

Ballet

Chapel

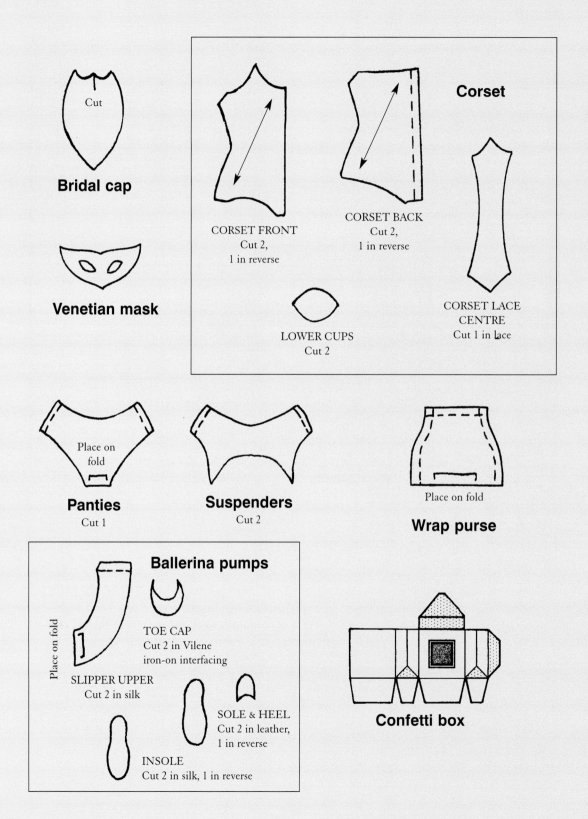

Bridal cap

Cut

Venetian mask

Corset

CORSET FRONT
Cut 2,
1 in reverse

CORSET BACK
Cut 2,
1 in reverse

CORSET LACE
CENTRE
Cut 1 in lace

LOWER CUPS
Cut 2

Panties
Cut 1

Place on fold

Suspenders
Cut 2

Wrap purse
Place on fold

Ballerina pumps

Place on fold

SLIPPER UPPER
Cut 2 in silk

TOE CAP
Cut 2 in Vilene
iron-on interfacing

SOLE & HEEL
Cut 2 in leather,
1 in reverse

INSOLE
Cut 2 in silk, 1 in reverse

Confetti box

About the Author

Sue developed an interest and love for art, embroidery and needlework from an early age and has continued to refine her skills.

After leaving school she trained in commercial art and store display while also practising dressmaking. Gradually she developed a love for the more ornate forms of dress: heirloom christening gowns, bridal and evening wear, and a passion for teddy bears resulted in the creation of some very special bridal bears.

Sue became interested in miniatures as a hobby and, following two years of contributing to *The Dolls' House Magazine* published by GMC, rekindled her love of 'all things bridal' in miniature.

Acknowledgements

I would like to say a very special thank you to Christiane Berridge whose support, encouragement and faith in my work led to the development of my business the Enchanted Cottage and the creation of this book.

Thank you also to all the dedicated miniaturists who, despite very busy commitments with their own miniature productions, came to my aid with kindness, enthusiasm and a sincere willingness to help me in my many hours of need. Many thanks to everyone at Katy Sue Dolls, Marc at Anglesey Dolls Houses, Sue Cook for her lovely plaster ware, Josephine Sladdin who sat at the end of the phone and catered to my every need and a dear friend Margaret Hodkinson who tirelessly made up my beautiful roses, waterlillies and ivy, and simply provided a shoulder to lean on when the need arose.

Heart-felt thanks also to the many customers and friends at the Enchanted Cottage who planted this particular seed in my head in the first place. I hope you have found this book entertaining, enjoyable and, ultimately, inspirational.

Suppliers

Gown fabrics and tulles, silk ribbons and roses, rose and bow makers, lace, trimmings and crystals, salon furniture plans, Swarovski crystal chandeliers and lighting fixtures, brass leaves, jewellery stands, Mini Mundus furniture kits, bespoke miniatures, parchment and packaging templates, miniature electric irons, and mannequins, sewing machine, stool and tiered workbaskets by Heidi Ott:

Sue Jo's Enchanted Cottage
79 Wellburn Road
Donwell Village
Washington
Tyne & Wear NE37 1DB
UK
Tel: +44 (0)191 4166411
www.suesenchantedcottage.co.uk

Building and garden components:

Anglesey Dolls' Houses
5A Penrhos Industrial Estate
Holyhead
Anglesey LL65 2UQ
UK
Tel. +44 (0)1407 761909
www.angleseydollshouses.co.uk

Parchment roses, paper petals and leaves:

Margaret Hodkinson
Foxglove Cottage
11 Holder Road
Maidenbower
Crawley
West Sussex RH10 7HL
UK
Tel: +44 (0)1293 888561

Doll kits:

Katy Sue Designs Ltd
Tedco Business Works
Henry Robson Way
South Shields
Tyne & Wear NE33 1RF
UK
Tel. +44 (0)191 4274571
www.katysuedolls.com

Doll wigs:

Josephine Sladdin
Leighton
Upper Sutherland Road
Lightcliffe
Halifax
West Yorkshire HX3 8NT
UK

Hat and wig stands:

Roger Baert
62 Bramley Lane
Hipperholme
Halifax
West Yorkshire HX3 8NS
UK

Plasterware:

Sue Cook Miniatures
Unit 5
Arundel Mews
Arundel Place
Brighton BN2 1GG
UK
Tel. +44 (0)1273 603054
www.suecookminiatures.com

Laser-cut arches, internal arched windows and wallpaper:

Hobby House
12 St Ronan's Road
Monkseaton
Whitley Bay NE25 8AX
UK
Tel: +44 (0)191 2902906

Variegated silk ribbon:
Little Trimmings
PO Box 2267
Reading RG4 8WG
UK
+44 (0)118 9473155
www.littletrimmings.com

Tiny shoes and leatherwear:
Susan Lee Miniatures
8 Springfields
Tetbury
Gloucestershire GL8 8EN
UK
Tel. +44 (0)1666 505936
www.susan-lee-miniatures.com

Lavender sprigs:
Veronica Ann Pickup
8 Dixon's Farm Mews
Preston Old Road
Clifton Village
NR Preston PR4 0PA
UK

Sheet and strip wood and
speciality woods:
Wood Supplies
Monkey Puzzle Cottage
53 Woodmansterne Lane
Wallington
Surrey SM6 0SW
UK
www.wood-supplies.com

Table lights:
Ray Storey Lighting
www.raystoreylighting.com

Cranberry glassware
(on hat stand, page 47):
Glasscraft www.glasscraftuk.com

Flower columns and urns:
Tee Pee Crafts
www.teepeecrafts.co.uk

Bridal boots and
point-toe shoes
(lower shelf of shoe display)
www.perrisminiatures.co.uk

Perfume and flower
girl baskets:
Chicken Little Miniatures
available from
www.collade.cco.uk

Perfumes and perfume displays:
Lisa's Little Things 15998, NW
94th Street, Topeka, Kansas
66617, USA
www.lisaslittlethings.com

Butterfly and Louis-style
chairs:
Judee Williamson & Nicole
Walton Marble available from
www.miniaturefloors.com

Hat collection:
By Nancy Manders available
from www.spminiatures.com

Bath salts:
Little Addictions available from:
www.minikitz.com

Toile pattern china (on bridal
counter, page 34):
www.Stokesayware.com

Trumpet sewing workbasket:
Cheviot Miniatures
Tel: +44 (0)1665 835259

Trunk:
The Luggage Lady
Sue Popley
Tel: +44 (0)1347 810634

Fabric dyes:
Dylon
www.dylon.com

Paints:
Dulux
www.dulux.co.uk
Winsor and Newton
www.winsornewton.com

Index

GMC Publications

Castle Place, 166 High Street, Lewes,
East Sussex BN7 1XU
United Kingdom

Tel: 01273 488005 Fax: 01273 402866
E-mail: pubs@thegmcgroup.com
Website: www.gmcbooks.com

Contact us for a complete catalogue, or visit our website.
Orders by credit card are accepted.